SMALL GROUP

**H
E
L
P**

GUIDES

Let's get started!

by
Dan Lentz

Standard
PUBLISHING

Let's Get Started!
Published by Standard Publishing,
Cincinnati, Ohio
www.standardpub.com

Produced by Susan Lingo Books™

14 13 12 11 10 09 08 07   9 8 7 6 5 4 3 2 1
978-0-7847-2073-8

DEDICATION

This book would have not been possible if it weren't for…

- *My wife Kim, my partner in all our small group ministry endeavors.*

- *Our kids—Sam, Katie, and Grace—who have taught me more about Christian community than all the small groups to which I have belonged.*

- *Michael Mack, my friend, my editor, and founder of SmallGroups.com.*

- *The Small Group Network, who have contributed articles and ideas.*

- *My family, for the love of Christ they have shown me.*

Contents

Small Groups— Why Bother?

LET'S GET STARTED!

That's the focus of this book—to gain some insights on starting small groups in your church or ministry. But if I said the only focus of this book is to start small groups, I'd be covering only part of the book's objective. Not only do we want to explore starting small groups, we want to explore starting small groups right! That makes my task as the author and your task as the reader a bit more challenging.

THINK ABOUT IT...

I have approached this topic from the standpoint that small groups are not what is missing from the church so much as small groups are the

As we take this journey into small groups together, I want you to know we are not alone. Jesus was a small group leader as well as a small group ministry starter, so that puts us in very good company! Small groups are not some current church fad or church growth strategy. From the beginning Christ followers have been meeting in relational community in small groups.

In This Chapter...

- Small groups are primary rather than supplementary in the church.
- A small group is simply a basic expression of the church.
- At its core, small groups are about relationships—with the Lord and one another.
- Senior church leaders are vital in embracing the values of Christian community.
- Knowing and living Christian community creates passion for small groups.

church in one of its many expressions. You will get the most out of this book by viewing small groups as an integral part of the church rather than just an add-on ministry program of the church.

Many small group books talk about the methods or philosophy of a particular church that has successful small groups. This book is not a story about one church's journey into small groups; rather, I want to empower you to design and implement methods that will serve your church and grow your Christian community in the way God is leading you to do it.

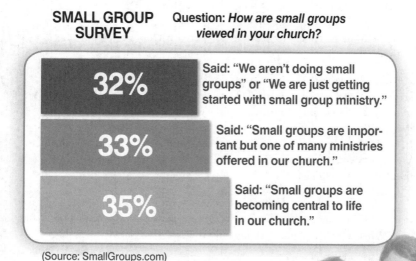

SMALL GROUP SURVEY

Question: *How are small groups viewed in your church?*

32% Said: "We aren't doing small groups" or "We are just getting started with small group ministry."

33% Said: "Small groups are important but one of many ministries offered in our church."

35% Said: "Small groups are becoming central to life in our church."

(Source: SmallGroups.com)

It is important for you to determine what effective small groups are and what they are not in your context. You will also discover along the way why some small group ministries thrive and why some do not.

Just as we are not alone in our small group ministry efforts, I have not been alone in compiling this book. I have distilled many resources and ideas from an army of small group ministry experts known as the *Small Group Network*. Over the years as both a member and now as director of this ministry, the Small Group Network, with its World Wide Web home at *http://SmallGroups.com*, has provided insights and ideas for this book.

WHAT IS A SMALL GROUP ANYWAY?

Look up! Look up! That's not a trite spiritual saying for me; it is practical. I have been an amateur astronomer most of my life. I enjoy exploring the wonders and mystery of the sky, weather, and outer space. Not long ago I was talking to another person in my small group about the rovers NASA sent to Mars to explore the surface of our neighbor planet. I was telling my friend that as I was watching the images being relayed back from the Mars rovers on my computer screen, I got a strange idea.

Say you are monitoring NASA's rovers on the surface of Mars. What if, instead of seeing an image of reddish colored dirt and rocks, you see the clear image of a "being," not a human being, but a being more like E.T.! He is holding a sign, which when translated reads, "Welcome earthlings! We have been studying your people and your ways. One thing we cannot figure out. *What is this thing called Christian small groups?"*

This illustration is obviously ridiculous, but the question is not. So I asked my friend, "If someone with little or no prior experience with small groups asked you, 'What is a small group?' what would you say?"

The "Acts" of the Early Small Group Members

Whenever I consider a question like *"What is a small group?"* I like to review a little background. When Jesus left the earth and ascended into Heaven (Acts 1:1-15), the disciples were left "looking intently up" into the sky in wonder and mystery. Rather than going their separate ways, those disciples gathered back together in an upper room in Jerusalem. Being together was the one thing they knew to do after spending these last few years together with Jesus. It was in the upper room that the next part of God's plan was set into motion.

"Then they returned to Jerusalem from the hill called the Mount of Olives, a Sabbath day's walk from the city. When they arrived, they went upstairs to the room where they were staying. ... They all joined together constantly in prayer, along with the women and Mary the mother of Jesus, and with his brothers."

— Acts 1:12-14

The coming of the Holy Spirit would empower these Christ-followers as they became the church. The church's mission centered on Jesus' last words to this first small group: *Make more and more baptized, obedient followers of Jesus Christ, both locally and throughout the earth.*

Now here is the key question: *What did Jesus leave behind for the fulfillment of his mission?*

➤ *Did he leave a headquarters building?* **No. The Israelites had a temple building that was the center of their worship, but Jesus said before he died that he would tear down the old temple and build a new one in three days (Matthew 26:61). This new temple would be spiritual, rather than bricks and mortar. And besides, within a few years, Christians weren't even welcome around the Jewish temple area.**

➤ *Did Jesus leave New Testament writings for churches to read and study?* **(Be careful!) No. The Old Testament Scriptures were widely available and read by early Christians, and some writings about Jesus' life were to be recorded shortly, but the earliest New Testament writings weren't circulated widely among churches until a few decades after Jesus ascended. While most of you reading this book enjoy having God's Word in the form of an abundance of printed Bibles, that was not the case with the early Christians.**

During those first few decades of rapid church growth and multiplication, what did Jesus leave for his message to be told and his mission to be fulfilled? It was a community of people filled with the Holy Spirit, and not a very large community of people at that. What transformed a few sinful and selfish individuals from sky-staring groupies to a world changing small group? *Christ's Holy Spirit.*

KEY CONCEPT

At its core, a small group is simply a group of Holy Spirit indwelt people who have intentional growing relationships with each other and with the Lord, and use those relationships to help fulfill Christ's mission for the church, while learning to love Jesus and one another at the same time. The essence of small groups is not much more complex than that!

Initially it's tempting to try and wrap a lot of other parameters around the definition of a small group: recommending the maximum number of people who can be in a group, establishing what the group agenda is, writing leadership criteria, determining the optimal frequency of small group gatherings, building a leader support/coaching structure, and more. These criteria can help a small group ministry grow and sustain spiritual health, but until you can embrace the simplicity of the early church pattern that a small group is people in mission-driven relationship to God and to one another, you will always have confusion in your church about the nature of small groups.

The temptation is to look at our non-relational traditions, buildings, worship services, and other church programs as the essence of what people need to grow to maturity and win others to Christ. These can all be very important to the overall function of the church, but without relational ministry we fall short of our calling as a Christian community.

TOP 10 — STRANGE THINGS YOUR NEIGHBORS MUST THINK YOUR SMALL GROUP IS...

10. A basket, cooking utensils, or resealable containers "cult."

9. Yep, it is definitely a cult! But they'll be gone as soon as the next comet comes by.

8. People are smiling and happy when they leave, so they must be sharing some form of mind-altering substance.

7. A stealth organizational meeting for a political party.

6. A front for a members-only bingo party.

5. Strangers keep showing up at the same house; it must be a witness protection program. I knew it!

4. I'm pretty sure we've been added to the neighborhood watch list. The same car drives by slowly every fifteen minutes during the meeting!

3. Steer clear. It's a "Network Marketing" party.

2. Everyone's carrying the same book. Must be the one I saw the other day on Oprah.

1. A fan club meeting to watch reruns of Desperate Housewives.

(Source: SmallGroups.com)

GOT SMALL GROUPS?

Interestingly enough, I don't know of a church that doesn't have small groups in one form or another. Lots of them don't have declared small group ministries, but people get into small groups regardless of whether small groups is an "official" ministry or not. People naturally and automatically seek out relationships. It's been said that if someone new to the church doesn't form a relationship with someone else within a few months, they are likely to leave the church or at best always be on the fringe.

Jesus didn't necessarily try to organize a small group ministry. Instead, he started a relational ministry that functioned in a small group. He then modeled and taught what it means to live in relationship to God and one another through his everyday life. Yes, Jesus participated in the Jewish synagogue activities, but his ministry was in the day-to-day activities of life.

Remember...

As you think about start-ing small groups, don't discount the natural small group relation-ships that already exist in your church. Part of creating Christian community is helping people see their existing relationships can revolve around the mission of the church. This, in turn, helps people use their routine daily rela-tional time with people for the glory of God.

> I no longer call you servants, be-cause a servant does not know his master's business. Instead, I have called you friends, for everything that I learned from my Father I have made known to you.
>
> —John 15:15

What does a Christ-centered small group do? The simple answer is that it lives in relationship to the Lord and to one another. God's Word dedicates a great deal of its content to this community. Consider the following passage:

"They joined with the other believ-ers and devoted themselves to the apostles' teaching and fellowship, sharing in the Lord's Supper and in prayer. A deep sense of awe came over them all, and the apostles performed many miraculous signs and wonders. And all the believers met together constantly and shared everything they had. They sold their possessions and shared the pro-ceeds with those in need. They worshiped together at the Temple each day, met in homes for the Lord's Supper, and shared their meals with great joy and generosity—all the while praising God and enjoying the goodwill of all the people. And each day the Lord added to their group those who were being saved" (Acts 2:42-47, NLT).

The results of this life together are that:

➤ *The body, the church, heals itself as it is fitted together in the community (Ephesians 4:11-16)*

➤ *Grace is administered in various forms (1 Peter 4:10)*

➤ *People are spurred on to love and good deeds (Hebrews 10:23-25)*

➤ *This biblical community creates a picture of Christ that non-believers see, and as a result, attracts more and more people to Jesus (John 17:20-23)*

I regularly share my life stories with you.

COMMUNITY DEVELOPMENT

You regularly share your life stories with me.

Over time, our life stories begin to look and sound a lot more like Jesus' life story.

Together we share the life story of Jesus Christ as it is told in God's Word.

Yes, there needs to be much prayer, intentionality, training, leader development, and structure building for community to have sustainable and healthy growth in churches. But make no mistake; the real goal of the small group movement is simply to provide the context for authentic biblical community to occur. We should not settle for anything less.

I Agree, But...

We won't ever know Jesus Christ as well as we could unless we are knit together with others.

You might agree with this basic description of small groups yet have doubts that this value of Christian community is shared by others in your church community. Settle the issue in your own mind and heart first. Is relational ministry in small groups an add-on program, one ministry among many, or part of the fabric of your overall church life? If you don't get clear on that, you will run into walls later. Even if you don't know yet where your church is on this value, at least make the issue clear with yourself before moving ahead. Otherwise, you may find it difficult to persevere through the hard work of starting small groups.

In Colossians 1:28–2:3, Paul said he worked very hard to achieve the goal of people being encouraged and knit together by strong ties of love. He said the result of this work, of this knitting people together, was that these relational ties would help people know Christ himself.

You and I won't ever know Jesus Christ as well as we could unless we are knit together with others. Remember: I share my life stories with you, and you share your life stories with me. Together, we share the life story of Jesus as revealed in Scripture. And, over time, our life stories start to sound a lot more like Jesus' life story.

THE "GET IT" FACTOR

Like the apostle Paul, you must have clarity about the importance of relational ministry in your own heart and be living it yourself, so you will be willing to work hard to declare it to others. When you have this clarity, then the next time you explain small groups to the "man from Mars," the gal who just visited your weekend worship service, your elder board, or the unbelieving next-door neighbor, you will be able to speak from experience and passion, and not just from information you got from a book or small group seminar.

Once you've shared the central importance of Christian community with your church, wouldn't it be nice if everyone just "got it" about relational community and figured out they need to be living it with the people in their spheres of influence? But people don't always automatically "get it."

If Christian community isn't already the culture in your church, then, unfortunately, people who have been around your church the longest sometimes have the hardest time "getting it." Newer Christians, who haven't established a lot of church paradigms yet, may get it more quickly and easily. Think about your church and analyze how small group relational values will be received by those in your congregation. Then approach the introduction of small group ministry accordingly.

CONFESSIONS OF A SMALL GROUP DIRECTOR

WATCH THE LANGUAGE!

I have found that a big key is to watch my language, both in personal conversations and public forums. I would never say the essence of church is a building, worship service, or set of traditions. But I have learned that when I constantly say I am "going" to church or involved in things "at" church or I ask someone "where" his church is located or what "time" church starts, I communicate that church is really about what happens in a specific building at a specific time each week. Everything else that happens in life, including family, vocation, and even small groups, is automatically seen as secondary to "doing church."

You might say it's just semantics, but your vocabulary indicates what you think and believe. Be clear about your paradigm; do you go to church or are you being the church? And how do small groups fit into that paradigm?

WHO NEEDS TO "GET IT" FIRST?

Opinions vary about who needs to be on the small group values page first: senior leaders, other key influencers in the church, or a group of grassroots Christ-followers? Some people start with a top-down approach (get senior leaders on board first), while others use a bottom-up approach (get a grassroots movement going first). It may be relatively easier to use a bottom-up approach where a few other grassroots people share and live this value together. But it is important to realize that the growth of Christian community in the church as a whole is tied to the "get it" factor of senior leaders.

• If you are a senior leader, you've started in the right place by reading this book! But don't just use a top-down approach. Get people involved and give them ownership early. The power of a small group movement is getting people involved in ministry at all levels.

• If you are not a senior leader, then you will need to develop a plan to help your senior leadership "get it." Of course, don't try to impose your values or manipulate, but be an encourager and supporter.

SMALL GROUP SURVEY

QUESTION: *How would you describe the senior leaders' commitment to building small group community in your church?*

Of churches surveyed who have been able to establish a small group ministry:

65% said, "Our senior leaders preach it and live it!"

14% said, "Our senior leaders preach it, but don't live it."

13% said, "Our senior leaders allow small groups, but don't actively support them"

3% said, "Our senior leaders don't support small groups at all; our groups are underground."

(Source: SmallGroups.com)

Small group growth and multiplication can happen organically at the grassroots level and produce wonderful fruit, but eventually growth, leader development, and ongoing leader support will hit walls if senior leaders aren't "on board" and encouraging the process to move forward.

On the other hand, evidence shows that where senior leaders are living and preaching the value of Christian community, the ministry has a better chance of getting started well and sustaining growth.

ASK AND ANSWER THE RIGHT QUESTIONS

Church leaders often begin by asking, "How do we start small group ministry in our church? How do we get everyone involved?" I think these are the wrong questions. More useful questions to pose and answer are:

Why do we want to start small groups?

Are small groups and church the same thing or different?

Are small groups integral to the overall life of a church in a similar way that our weekly worship service is integral to the life of the church?

When it comes to relational ministry, are church leaders willing to preach it and live it?

These questions help clarify the value of small groups in the overall ministry structure of your church. Are small groups to be part of the fabric of the church or one ministry among many?

Prior to launching groups among your church, use these questions to clarify the role of small groups, and more specifically, the role of Christian community. Otherwise, when conflict and competition start to crowd out the values of Christian community, you may easily give in or give up when it comes to making Christian community a part of the fabric of your congregation.

KNOWING VS. BEING

As you help others embrace Christian community values, teach them these values but also help them experience these values. Read and study key sections of Scripture like *John 17; Acts 2:42-47; Colossians 1:28–2:3; 2 Corinthians 6:11-13; Ephesians 4:11-16; 1 Peter 4:7-10.* But to study and meditate on these passages and not live them would be only an academic exercise.

For more help starting a leadership small group ("Turbo Group"), search for articles on the topic at www.SmallGroups.com.

Once you have spent time experiencing Christian community and doing relational ministry with other key people in your church, you've taken a great first step! At that point you will also have the lifestyle that models the value of Christian community rather than only the knowledge of Christian community. Now it is time to make some key decisions. More about that in the next chapter.

c a u t i o n

I have sat with groups where we thoroughly researched and discussed biblical Christian community values and had strong agreement on those values. And yet, because those key leaders had not experienced that community themselves, when we came upon critical decisions of resource allocation or ministry program competition issues, it was clear they had not fully embraced Christian community values, because they had not lived it. They knew it, but just weren't passionate about it.

TEN THINGS I WOULD DO DIFFERENTLY IF I WERE STARTING A SMALL GROUP MINISTRY TODAY

(The following is from Dan Smith, SmallGroups.com.)

❶ I would answer the "why" questions first.

Even though I was warned by every book and speaker to change values before attempting to change structure, I still tried to implement structural change first. This had several detrimental side effects, including:

- *losing members who resisted the change simply because they did not understand the reasoning behind the shift*

- *continual backtracking, sidetracking, and back-filling as my understanding of small groups grew*

- *heightened fear from those in the congregation who couldn't see the method behind the madness*

❷ I would be more careful in leader selection.

One of the first small groups I established was filled with hand-picked leaders. It collapsed within two months, and many of those initial leaders ended up leaving the church at some point during the transition. I had chosen those initial leaders from a program-generated criteria; I looked for people who could "make it happen." During that same time period, I pointed out one woman in the church to my wife and sagely declared, *"She will never be a leader in this church."* That woman later became a small group leader, small group area director, and is now considering a call to become a small group pastor on staff. She is not a "make it happen" kind of person but is highly relational. She knows how to listen to God and listen to people.

❸ I would pray and look for "called" leadership.

If someone leads because I have recruited them, they will not last over the long haul. If someone leads because God has recruited them, they will grow stronger by the year. When trouble comes (and it always does), it is much more effective to appeal to their call to God rather than their commitment to me or the organization.

❹ I would start with one (count 'em, one) prototype group.

We began our transition with three groups. I was in a hurry to get as many people involved as quickly as possible. This created an uneven small group experience and value base that we are still trying to overcome three years later. As the small groups began to multiply, some became good at community, some prayer, and some evangelism. None were functional in all areas of group life. The small groups must start from a single source of vision if they are to be replicated with any sort of consistency.

❺ I would get used to conflict and confrontation much more quickly.

Not being a person who enjoys conflict, I treated this aspect of group life as an anomaly rather than the norm. The more I ignored the reality of conflict, the more prevalent it became. The truth is that small groups do not solve problems in the church; they only bring them out into the open! Especially in the first year of small group ministry, I found myself in a constant values conflict with just about everyone in the church.

Learning to speak the truth in love was the single greatest challenge of transitioning.

The truth is that small groups do not solve problems in the church; they only bring them out into the open!

❻ I would build relationships with nonbelievers.

Actually, I did this right, but it was more by God's grace than my design. About a year before beginning the transition, I became a volunteer police chaplain. In exchange for about twenty hours a month, I received a mission field that yields continual opportunities for evangelism, a base for modeling outreach, and a source for countless sermon illustrations. Church planters usually have to work in secular positions for financial reasons, but I think those of us in "full-time" ministry would gain a lot to be able to show our people how to reach the lost as opposed to just telling them how they should be doing it.

❼ I would emphasize hospitality more and events less.

One time, about a year into the transition, I decided my small group needed an outreach event. The plan was to show a Christian video in a rented facility on campus and invite our nonbelieving friends. I sacrificed devotional time, family time, and sermon preparation time organizing this thing. The night of the presentation no one (not even me) brought any nonbelievers. We ended up watching *"The Lion King."* I realize now I had just taken a programmed event and miniaturized it for our small group. The outcome was similar. Now we just open our homes for "Matthew Parties" (see Matthew 9:9-13). They are much cheaper and many times more effective.

❽ I would redefine success.

When we began transitioning, I end-loaded success. I thought and communicated that we would be successful only when we were fully transitioned and multiplying small groups like factory clockwork. The result was a feeling that success was always just a few steps ahead of where we were: the next multiplication, the next numerical barrier broken. The truth is that a church can be just as successful in God's eyes with two small groups as with 2,000 groups. If I do it again, I am going to have more fun right where I am.

❾ I would worry less and trust God more.

When we started:

- *I was afraid finances would collapse. They went up.*

- *I was afraid people would leave the church.*
  They did, but for every one who left two more came in.

- *I was afraid we wouldn't have enough leaders. At this time we have more trained leaders than small groups for them to lead.*

- *I was afraid people wouldn't join the groups. We have nearly 100% participation.*

❿ I would pray more.

When we first started small group ministry in the church, my assistant and I kept a prayer log for about 6 months. I averaged about 25 minutes a day in prayer. I considered myself a praying pastor. My personal planner shows that last week I prayed over 15 hours in seven days, and I still yearn for more time alone with God. This is quite a dramatic change for me in three years. How did it happen? I learned the little secret of small group ministry. Unlike a program-based design, it simply cannot work without lots and lots and lots of prayer.

Think About It

David Yonggi Cho, senior pastor of Yoido Full Gospel Church in Seoul, Korea, says if anyone would show him how to grow a church without prayer, he would "jump and shout." Until then he continues praying three hours a day. His congregation numbers 800,000 and counting and has more than 25,000 small groups. When my prayer life grows up, I want it to be like his.

(Source: D. S., SmallGroups.com)

The Big Decisions

Once you get your biblical community values established and are ready to begin small groups, it's time to sit down with the other folks and do some planning. The goal of the planning process is to use collaboration and consensus to create a unified plan that key planners and stakeholders work on together (*collaboration*) and that everyone can get behind (*consensus*).

✓ In This Chapter...

- The Planning Process & Planning Pitfalls
- Knowing the Difference Between Values, Strategies, Tactics, & Models
- Deciding Trasition Strategies
- What Does It Look Like In Real Life?

This planning may involve a staff team, senior leadership group, or ministry team/committee. Regardless of who is on the planning group, it is important that this group "gets it" with respect to biblical community values. Involving several folks who don't get it can be detrimental to the planning process.

Even when the planning group is unified on biblical community values, the small group ministry start-up planning is challenging enough.

WHEN A PLAN COMES TOGETHER

Hopefully, you have experienced biblical community prior to reading this book. Perhaps you started a new small group and used a great new curriculum to get it going. Everyone loved it. People grew. The group grew. Things went great…at least for a while.

Now it's time to figure out how to transfer your knowledge and experience with biblical community to the "many." The "many" are sometimes a diverse group of people: builder generation, boomer generation, buster generation, young people, singles, couples, empty nesters, elderly, and so on. Will this work the same way with all these diverse people? And what if problems arise, because they always do!

So you are planning, and what starts as a simple discussion becomes a major challenge. At first, the initial plan includes vision, a program, or a campaign that gets things started. Typically, this process starts with anticipation and excitement. But then, just as you think you've got the start-up process figured out, stuff happens like unexpected rapid growth or no growth or conflict or leadership problems or sin or unexpected attacks from the enemy. All of a sudden, your plans that seemed so great now seem inadequate and incomplete.

CONFESSIONS OF A SMALL GROUP DIRECTOR

THE CHILD CARE DILEMMA

Our small group planning team met to talk about an issue we were facing. Here's how the conversation went:

Steve: So far, we have envisioned that when small groups meet, parents of young children would individually make arrangements for their own child care. However, I've been approached by several parents who say weekly child care expenses will be a financial strain on them, or they don't have access to child care on weekday evenings. They wonder if child care could be provided at the small group site, provided all the church child care worker safety guidelines are met.

(Several on the planning team acknowledge similar conversations with parents.)

Fred: I don't think this is a good idea because most host homes are not set up to accommodate a bunch of kids.

Janice: Besides, how in the world can we insure the kind of child safety that we have here on the church campus?

Beth: Maybe we should see if small groups with young children can meet at the church building. Then there would be plenty of room for adults and kids and safety as well.

Jennifer: I think most people would prefer the atmosphere of a house rather than the church building for small group gatherings. But if expense is the main issue, then I don't see why the church couldn't help pay for child care expenses, since small groups are an official church activity.

(A couple of team members agree with this idea, but then...)

Bob: We have way too many programs at church that separate parents from kids. Maybe small groups shouldn't be another one of those activities. What do you think about including our kids in group time—actually have them be part of our small groups?

(Muffled groans are heard.)

Janice: We've gone way past time, and I need to get home to relieve my babysitter!"

(Source: SmallGroups.com)

What do you do in these situations? For sure, you pray! It's the first thing, last thing, and sometimes the only thing you can do. **Pray.**

The other thing you do, typically, is to continue to get the planning group involved in fine-tuning the plan. This is where it can get challenging!

It is precisely in these meetings that plans can get confusing and discussions can seem to go nowhere. You hope and pray plans come together, but sometimes they don't.

One thing that will be tested right away will be the strength of your planning group's community. Sometimes your greatest insights about leading a small group movement come from experiencing tensions and working through them in that leadership community. Don't shrink away from this conflict and tension. You will not be able to lead people to a place you have not been yourself, so accept these leadership challenges joyfully. But also, use this as an opportunity to learn some beneficial ways to handle and facilitate discussions such as these.

THE CRITICAL DIFFERENCE BETWEEN VALUES, STRATEGY, AND TACTICS WHEN PLANNING

Aside from keeping biblical community as the leading value of the planning team members, you can improve these discussions by focusing attention on one of three main areas at a time. Those three areas are values, strategies, and tactics. Now, lest you think you have to become a company executive or military strategist to figure out what I'm talking about, let me say it another way. Your planning sessions will go much better if you focus your discussion at one of three altitudes, one at a time. Those altitudes are: the *10,000-foot level* (values), *the 500-foot level* (strategies), and *eye-level* (tactics).

There is no question that to do adequate planning you have to spend time flying at each of the three altitudes. In the child care discussion you read earlier, people were flying at all different altitudes at the same time. When you dive and climb through all the different altitudes so often, your team becomes disoriented and unable to see anything clearly. So the remedy is to start at one altitude, get the lay of the land, and then move to another altitude gradually.

THE 10,000-FOOT LEVEL—VALUES

When you're on an airplane at high altitude and you look at the earth below, it's hard to make out details. You can see large major features like mountains and large rivers, but it is difficult to see details like houses and cars.

Likewise, values are closely held and worthwhile beliefs, principles, or standards that people should be able to see easily. Values remain relatively unchanged despite the details of the situation. Most times, it is good to start your discussion at this level because you can determine nonnegotiables that will drive your strategy (500-foot) and tactics (eye-level) decisions.

In the child care discussion, for example, the person who brought up the issue of child safety and the team leader who brought up the issue of parent-child spiritual discipleship were really bringing up issues related to values.

Values-level discussions often focus on scriptural principles and core beliefs. The key to keeping things at the values level is to guide the group by asking questions about the group's mission, vision, and core beliefs relative to the issue being discussed. When someone makes a comment that clearly seems to be more details-oriented than values-oriented, make a note of it, but defer these comments until later in your discussion.

Once you reach consensus about specific values, repeat what you have agreed upon so everyone hears and agrees before moving on.

—Source: SmallGroups.com

THE 500-FOOT LEVEL—STRATEGIES

As the airliner makes its approach to land, a lot of details come into view. Still, many things look small, but you can clearly see roads and runways. Using navigation resources and landmarks, you can begin to map out your approach to the landing point.

At this level you discuss and develop strategies that align with your values. A strategy is an approach to solving a problem or achieving an objective using whatever resources are available to make it work as effectively as possible.

In our child care discussion, once the group determined nonnegotiable values, the leader could have invited them to share ideas for how child care could be arranged. For instance, if the group determined the value of family discipleship should be an emphasized aspect of small groups, then one strategy would have been to have children and adults both at the site of the small group gathering with parents involved in some aspects of child care and the kids involved in some aspect of group life (specific involvement ideas would be saved for the eye-level tactics discussion).

On the other hand, if they decided the value was individual child safety, but child involvement in the group was not a high value, then one strategy might have been to continue to leave child care up to parents individually, in which case known babysitters and a known home environment exist. This, of course, seems to go against the original reason the child care situation was brought up (financial and logistical burdens on individuals). But if the values and strategy are confirmed to be sound, then details such as child care expenses can be most effectively dealt with at the eye-level (tactics) discussion.

At this point it is important to summarize the strategy the group has reached consensus about so everyone hears and agrees before moving on.

—Source: SmallGroups.com

EYE-LEVEL—TACTICS

Once your airliner is ready to touch down, the pilot performs a set of specific steps to insure a successful landing: landing gear down, flaps up, nose up, and so forth.

Likewise, tactics are detailed maneuvers to achieve the objectives set by strategy, which in turn support the values. At this level details are finally discussed and decisions made based on the unique circumstances of your situation and the strategy chosen.

In our child care example, let's say child safety and adult-only community time were high values. The group then discussed strategies and decided that parents would continue to be responsible for their own child care. Now they would discuss how to subsidize that child care so the burden would not be too great for any one family. At this point, tactics—such as having small groups start a joint small group child care fund or seeing if the larger church could help fund child care—would be open for discussion.

Realistically, many tactical decisions can probably be left up to the small groups themselves. Your planning goal is not to make all decisions for the groups, but to help set a course that can assure that the individual small groups retain the church's values and be reproducible.

Hopefully, by this point in the conversation, issues of values and strategy have been discussed. So if confusing comments emerge questioning the values or strategies previously selected, you would simply go back to your summarizing points for both discussions and ask, "Are these values and strategies what we agreed to? Or do we need to spend more time at one of these levels before moving on?"

—Source: SmallGroups.com

The end result of facilitating the discussion using the approach of values, strategy, and tactics may not make the discussion go more quickly, but typically a more effective process is in place and more ministry will result. It won't eliminate those confusing areas where values, strategies, and tactics seem to overlap, but in general, keeping your planning focused on one area at a time will help. Because don't you just love it when a plan comes together?

PLANNING AND SMALL GROUP MODELS

What does all this have to do with small group models? A model is simply the structure into which values, strategies, and tactics fit.

Churches actively pursuing small group ministry, intentionally or unintentionally, choose an organizational structure and system that provides a framework for group purpose, growth, outreach, leader development, ongoing leader support, and group multiplication. The framework or system that a church uses to accomplish these small group functions is sometimes called a "small group ministry model."

KEY CONCEPT

Your planning goal is not to make every decision for your group, but to help set a course that can assure your group retains the church's values.

Many churches fall into the temptation of choosing a model for their small group ministry that another successful church has made popular without first establishing small group ministry values. Another church's model and experience can be helpful, but they are rarely completely transferable. Adopting a model without getting clear on values can create confusion and added frustration as time goes on.

There is no one "right" small group ministry model. Every church needs to determine, and periodically redetermine, the right small group ministry model for its situation. Most small group ministries are hybrids of two or more models. Churches need to seek the model that supports their values and includes the most optimal strategies and tactics for their situation.

Definitions

Values: *the guiding principles and beliefs that drive all your other decisions. These are typically based on Scripture and your vision, and they remain relatively unchanged for the long term.*

Example: Spiritual growth is not optional for small group members.

STRATEGY: the approach or core practices you use to make your values a reality. Strategies typically involve medium- to long-term plans of how you will accomplish your objectives and goals.

Example: Small groups will participate in one church-wide spiritual growth campaign each year. Small groups will be supported through this campaign by under-shepherds and senior leaders within the structure of the small group ministry model.

TACTICS: the detailed activities that happen within your strategy. Tactics are sometimes only short-term ideas and can be changed as frequently as necessary.

Example: During the spiritual growth campaign, groups will use an agenda based around the pastor's sermon for that week.

MODEL: the organizational structure that supports your values, strategy, and tactics. Many models include some strategies and tactics. A model should be adapted for a particular ministry situation.

Example: A discipleship and shepherding pyramid with senior leaders mentoring and supporting under-shepherds, who are in turn coach and support small group leaders, who then lead, model, and support their small group members.

TRANSITION DECISIONS: MINISTRY MAKEOVER VS. NEW CONSTRUCTION

As you discuss and plan your values, strategies, tactics, and models, you should think about and plan how you will implement these ideas and activities. Do you gradually launch the ministry with a slow transition, or do you launch with a big splash and make changes more rapidly?

There are many ways to launch small groups initially, but during the planning process two start-up strategies in particular highlight the decisions that small group directors and church leaders face.

STRATEGY 1:
PROTOTYPE START-UP

One transition strategy is to start with some handpicked folks in one or a few pilot groups (sometimes called turbo groups) and focus on biblical community, outreach, leadership development, and group health. Live life together for a while and then send these first group members out to start recruiting and leading their own groups with the vision that this process of growing, reproducing, and multiplying will continue over time.

STRATEGY 2:
CAMPAIGN DRIVEN- START-UP

Another strategy launches small groups using a campaign or program as a catalyst. It gets a lot of people connected quickly, utilizing a curriculum that requires minimal leadership training up front.

Some say Strategy 1 emphasizes quality and group health at the expense of quantity—allowing only a few to enter community at first. And while it is true that this method does have a much flatter growth curve at first, quantity growth can increase rapidly as leadership multiplication continues through a few generations of groups and leaders. While this method certainly requires the ongoing training of leaders, much of the training is built into the structure. Because of this, a highly developed centralized training system is not as critical, since much of it happens organically through apprenticeship. In addition, group leader coaches and overseers naturally develop from the system rather than needing to be forced into it. One of the downsides of this strategy is that those outside the group process can see those inside as being exclusive or cliquish. In some cases if healthy practices are not passed on, the group will become ingrown, stagnant, and nonreproductive.

On the other hand, campaign-driven programs (Strategy 2), by their very nature, emphasize quantity, making small group connections available to many people all at once. Campaigns involve the whole church or at least significant segments of it. They generally use a specific curriculum that everyone uses simultaneously. This common purpose has the potential to build momentum, create church-wide excitement, and unify group vision. In this method many new leaders or hosts are required who typically have little or no prior experience with group leadership. Oversight and follow-up of these new groups and leaders needs to be more centralized and is more challenging because any prior small group leader support structure is typically undersized or nonexistent.

Discuss and plan values, strategies, tactics, and models, and how you will implement them.

TOP 10

WORST PROMOTIONAL SLOGANS FOR THE CHURCH'S SMALL GROUP MINISTRY

10. Small Groups: Be there or be square!

9. Small Groups: Where everybody knows something about your most embarrassing moments.

8. Small Groups: You can join one. We can help.

7. Don't be lame. Get in the game, and join a small group!

6. This ain't your momma's group!

5. Don't struggle alone. Come share your sins with us.

4. Small Groups: You can't try just one.

3. Small Groups: Better than your favorite TV show.

2. Small Groups: Learn how to forgive and reconcile through actual experience in someone's living room.

1. Small Groups: The snacks make it worthwhile!

(Source: SmallGroups.com)

Group health is also more of a concern because in some cases leaders have not had healthy biblical community modeled for them. This can lead to many groups shutting down after the campaign is over and folks having misconceptions about what biblical community in a small group is really like. There is a danger that even groups who stay together never really embrace some aspects of healthy biblical community, which leads once again to exclusiveness and stunted growth.

So what do you do? Quickly start lots of groups that get a lot of people connected into community and do the best you can on leadership quality and group health? Or start slow and develop a few groups with some handpicked folks who focus on leadership development and hope the model continues to multiply and increase quantity? Is one strategy right? Do you really have to decide between quality and quantity?

CONFESSIONS OF A SMALL GROUP DIRECTOR

CAMPAIGN START-UP

Several years ago, I used a 50-Day Spiritual Adventure (www.sunday-solutions.com) at our church to launch a small group ministry and get a few hundred folks into groups all at one time. The 50-Day Spiritual Adventure was a forerunner of the more recent 40 Days of Purpose (www.purposedriven.com) campaign. Many of the mechanics of the programs are the same. When done well, many folks make a commitment to be in small groups and enter into the life-changing pathway of biblical community.

More recently I've been involved in a church model in which we are starting groups more slowly by focusing on building quality first, starting with a single group and now growing to several groups through multiplication. The growth has been slow but steady. The spiritual growth and health have been exciting. I've seen leadership develop character and competency in significant ways through this approach.

Having been involved with both, I know that both approaches have their challenges and advantages. Both approaches have the potential to lead many into a life-changing Christian community. Both have specific weaknesses and strengths in either quantity or quality.

And if you don't think through the strengths and weaknesses and try to address them, I can tell you from experience that what you start with most times is what you finish with. In other words, the values you instill at the beginning of either of these two strategies are typically the values you will have when you finish. The old "bait-and-switch" doesn't work very well most times.

For instance, if you emphasize quantity—that everyone should be in a small group and that the group experience will take care of itself through curriculum or whatever program you use, then the quantity value seems to always be instilled in your people. When people discover that group health and leader development are suffering, they commonly respond, *"Hey, don't worry too much; things are still working because we've still got a lot of people in groups!"*

On the other hand, if you emphasize quality only—that what happens in the group experience is more important than how many people are in groups—then new people are perceived as damaging to the group dynamics, and potential apprentice leaders never get to the point of feeling qualified and empowered to lead. The common response is: *"Hey, we are not ready to add people or multiply yet; we need to learn how to grow more first."*

—Source: SmallGroups.com

By now I hope you have realized the important question is not about whether to choose quantity or quality in your small group approach. The real decision is how to provide an environment where quality and quantity are valued from the start, regardless of the method or strategy you select. It's not "either-or"; it should be "both-and."

Here are some critical factors that can help quantity and quality coexist from start to finish in your small groups:

Prayer. In research conducted on what factors and skills contribute most to small group growth both in quality and quantity, the leading factor is leaders who pray daily for their small groups.

Leadership Community. Bring your leaders into an environment of community themselves for several weeks or months prior to leading their groups, or have leaders meet in a leadership huddle regularly while they are leading a group. Get leaders away on a retreat occasionally to experience defining moments of community. Keep ratios of the care of staff and coaches to group leaders in the range of 1:3 to 1:5, even if it means having fewer groups. Don't let other competing ministry activities crowd out leaders' time to be involved in the lives of group members.

Reproducible Values and Mission. Keep group values and mission simple and reproducible. If group leaders don't have a firm sense of why they are doing what they are doing, they will find it difficult to sustain momentum over the long haul. Without the right underlying values, the inevitable struggles and problems that come up in group life will cause many members and leaders to "check out" of the process.

Commitment to Relational Ministry. Much of the New Testament is written in the context of churches meeting in homes with people in close relationship to one another. It is not surprising then that much of the New Testament instruction is of a relational nature. Consider the "one anothers" of Scripture. Quality happens when we follow these instructions faithfully and lovingly. It means some groups may need to go on life support or be shut down, particularly if they are isolated and unhealthy. If a group or leader is doing more harm than good and does not have a submissive spirit, then we must value quality over quantity.

(Source: SmallGroups.com)

Two values that drive longer-term group quantity and quality that always tend to slip off the radar screen are *outreach* and *multiplication*. Research shows that outreach and assimilation of new people into the group actually improves the quality of a group over the long term, contrary to what is popularly thought. Outreach leads to group quality, and multiplication will increase the quantity of groups. Group multiplication almost never happens spontaneously in a group. Leaders and groups need to have the vision and processes of multiplication reintroduced over and over. Don't wait to emphasize these two values "later." Emphasize them from the start.

Regardless of what approach you take to launch new small groups, quantity and quality will result if you focus on these issues.

CASE STUDY

How a Church Launched a Small Group Ministry

(Source: SmallGroups.com)

About 30 years after a medium-size church had been planted, the leaders of the church recognized they had a crowd but little community. As a result of this evaluation, they felt the church needed to grow smaller as it grew larger. Senior leaders then developed a Small Group Ministry Vision. The vision was to connect everyone in the church to a small group for discipleship and care. The original vision also included transforming staff and elders to senior shepherds, small group leaders, or coaches of small group leaders, even though few of the elders had previous small group leadership experience.

Because the senior minister already had too much responsibility on his plate, a small groups director was hired from within the congregation to oversee and be the point person for the small group ministry effort.

The leadership decided on five values, represented by the acronym FLOWS: Fellowship, Learning, Outreach, Worship, and Service.

F Fellowship

The elders and staff launched a short-term pilot small group early in the process. It was initially designed to be a turbo group of sorts that would orient, train, and prepare the elders to launch small groups of their own once the pilot group was completed.

L Learning

O Outreach

W Worship

It was decided groups would be initially formed around existing relationships, encouraging people to form groups who already had other relational connections to the group leader, rather than form groups through random assignments. Those not connected through preexisting relationships would be assigned to a group (group leader) to be prayed for and invited to the group.

S Service

Each regular smaller group gathering of the church (midweek Bible studies, Sunday school, ministry teams) were highly encouraged to incorporate the values and activities of FLOWS. However, groups and group leaders had independence to develop their own meeting agendas and to select learning and serving focuses.

To build momentum for the effort, leadership decided in the first year of the small group ministry effort to use a campaign-style program to accelerate the launch of new small groups among adults in the congregation.

New group leaders were recruited and received a total of six hours of training leading up to the campaign. Every new group leader was charged with:

➤ *Monitoring and facilitating the activities of Fellowship, Learning, Outreach, and Worship during the group meetings*

➤ *Praying for and making contact with group members outside of group meetings*

➤ *Reaching out and inviting new people into the group (both disconnected churchgoers and the unchurched)*

➤ *Raising up and training an apprentice leader*

➤ *Preparing the group for multiplication into two or more groups*

Let's Get Started! 33

The campaign was completed, and about an equal number of Sunday school groups and midweek groups met throughout the campaign period. After the campaign, a gathering to debrief the group leaders was held, and approximately 90% of the groups agreed to keep meeting.

The first time the campaign was used, the result was a significant increase in small group participation. At the peak, more than 60% of average weekend worship attendance regularly participated in a small group. Small group involvement then plateaued at this level and eventually began a slight decline over the next two years.

Several reasons have been identified for stagnation of new involvement and spiritual health concerns:

➤ *The Leader Support System.* The campaign started with nearly forty new small group leaders (including Sunday school group leaders) and no relational coaching structure except for staff. In the beginning the elders were going to function more in coaching roles, but their lack of group experience and their particular mix of gifts made the elders ineffective in coaching roles. A group of gifted coaches was eventually recruited, but each of these individuals also led his or her own small group in addition to many other leadership roles in the church. The revamped coaching system was not effective at leader support.

➤ *Program Competition.* The church has several ongoing programs that require much time and energy both from staff and volunteers. Most small group leaders were also heavily involved in other programs, boards, and committees, which diminished the time and energy they could invest in relationships with group members.

➤ *Resistance to Group Multiplication.* Few small groups were ever able to successfully birth a new leader or group. Some larger groups, where long-term relationships already existed, were hostile to multiplying, which made larger groups difficult to manage for leaders. This created a culture where some groups began valuing comfort and complacency over mission and outreach.

➤ *Reliance on Programmed Group Methods Rather Than Relational Methods.* Because many of the groups had started during the campaign program, it was difficult to build momentum outside the "programmed environment." The church used a second and third campaign two and four years after the first one. The goal was to boost momentum for small groups, although the benefit from later campaigns was not nearly as great as the initial campaign.

➤ *Point Leader Absence.* After four years in his position, the staff small groups director left to help lead a new church plant the mother church sponsored. For a variety of reasons, the elders and staff decided not to fill this position with another paid staff member, and so existing small groups were covered by volunteers and the already thinly spread remaining staff.

Lessons Learned

➤ When trying to build a small group ministry, the coordinated and unified effort of all key leaders is very important.

➤ If the small group director had it to do over again, he would start slower and perhaps delay using a campaign until a base of experienced small group leaders was better established, possibly through more turbo-grouping.

Questions to Ask

• *Is what we are doing now essential in fulfilling our calling to make disciples, or do we feel that we can and should go to another level, even if it requires the church to choose a new model?*

• *Is the biblical community values of F.L.O.W.S. able to be applied to all group gatherings including Sunday school, midweek Bible studies, ministry teams, choirs, building committees, and other groups?*

• *Do we as a leadership group see ourselves as a model of relational ministry for the rest of the congregation?*

Churches with between **40–60%** of adult worshipers enrolled in small groups are the most common type of North American church that has a declared small group program. The fundamental characteristic of these churches is that a single staff member is responsible for the small group ministry of the church.

Besides being responsible for small groups, this staff member typically has additional ministry responsibilities. In most cases, a staff person with the declared small group assignment will get twice the participation that a layperson will, simply because of the time and energy he or she has to put into it. This is the single biggest difference between churches at the **20%** small group participation plateau and churches at the 50–60% level.

Another key characteristic of this plateau is choosing small group leaders from the existing leadership pool. Typically, these leaders are already over-involved, limiting their effectiveness in small group ministry. There are two major distinguishing characteristics of churches with **more than 80%** small group participation, both related to staffing.

Carl George writes, *"If the senior leadership of the church says, 'We want all the staff to develop leadership for the small group system,' you can push the percentage up another 20%."* The involvement of multiple staff in group oversight is a significant difference from churches at the **50% level** (single staff person overseeing groups) or the **20% level** (volunteer oversight of groups).

DECISION-MAKING NEVER ENDS

As you can see, you have no shortage of decisions to think about as you begin a small group ministry. But the truth is you won't know the bulk of the decisions you need to make until you get into it. So make the foundational decisions you need to make to get things started.

Of course, once you have your initial plan, the next task will begin to loom large on your radar screen. And that task is identifying leaders of your small groups. That will be the topic of the next chapter.

What Your Groups Can't Do Without: Leaders

Let's say you have worked through some basic components of values and have begun thinking and praying through strategies and tactics. One key component of this process will include small group *leadership*. Small group leadership is such a critical issue that it requires much of your attention as you get started.

The first thing to be really clear about is that Jesus is the real small group leader. He simply uses Holy Spirit indwelt people as his hands, feet, voice, and body, with each part doing its own special work, helping the other parts grow, so that the whole small group is healthy and growing and full of love (see Ephesians 4:16).

Knowing that Jesus is the true small group leader should be reassuring to anyone involved in the small group leader-selection process. With that in mind you need to look for potential group leaders who are the most willing to allow Jesus to use them. This does not mean you necessarily look for the most qualified people to lead small groups; rather, you seek people who God is calling to lead.

CONSIDER THIS...

The life force of a small group comes from Christ empowering it—Christ in the midst, indwelling it. He is the catalyst directing your small group how to grow and what to do. Christ must lead the small group. Beware of thinking too highly of yourself. You are a servant who facilitates the group so they can experience the life of Christ flowing into them for healing and restoration. Your small group members must also sense his presence guiding them into ministry to the unreached people around them.

—Source: Ralph Neighbour, Jr., SmallGroups.com

CONFESSIONS OF A SMALL GROUP DIRECTOR

When Katie asked to get together to talk about small groups, I readily agreed. She was bright and perceptive, an excellent leader, but that is not what her body language conveyed. Her shoulders drooped, her eyes were dull, and her face was blank as she shoved a paper across the desk toward me. "We had our small group kick-off meeting last night, and then I got this from you—another list of expectations." Sighing deeply she said, "I don't know if I can go on."

As I listened, my mind flashed back to an earlier conversation with Steve, another small group leader. His demeanor stood in sharp contrast to Katie's. A bright smile lit his face as he talked about his small group. In fact, he glowed. "I love my small group," he confessed. "And I appreciate you and the church leadership challenging me to make a difference in other people's lives. I know you pray for me daily. It's a challenging role that you have asked me to fill, but with the Lord and your help, I know we can do it."

The most notable difference between Katie and Steve was how valued they felt as individuals. Katie felt weighed down by her church's expectation for the growth of the small group program; Steve felt uplifted by his church's care and concern for him and his group members' spiritual growth. Katie felt the pressure to conform and comply with programs and positions. Steve experienced the freedom and empowerment to pursue what God was blessing and to put people and biblical community principles first.

Small groups are about people. Small group leaders need to know that their spiritual growth, as well as that of their group members, comes before the growth of any program or ministry. Small groups are primarily organic—living, breathing, and dynamic—not organizational. Organization is important, but the structure needs to serve people, not people the structure. Small groups are organic, fluid, flexible, and complex. The growth of a small group program is an outcome of the spiritual growth of the people in it.

—Source: Betty Veldman Wieland , SmallGroups.com

Many times an untrained group leader with a willing heart is more desirable than someone who seems gifted but is less teachable. Small group leadership skills and knowledge can be produced through training and a willing heart. A teachable spirit, however, is more difficult to produce.

The Bible provides many principles for selecting and screening leaders. The following is adapted from an article by Steven Reames on SmallGroups.com.

METHODS FOR LEADER SELECTION

❶ *God raises up*: "While they were worshiping the Lord and fasting, the Holy Spirit said, 'Set apart for me Barnabas and Saul for the work to which I have called them'" (Acts 13:2). God is sovereign, and we should not oppose whom he calls.

CHECK THIS OUT!

If church leaders need to buy into small groups, do they also need to lead them? It has been said that church leadership shouldn't be targeted to be small group leaders because they aren't always the right people for the job. But it has also been said that small group leaders tend to come from the same pool of people who do everything else in church (which are typically church leaders!). I can help you solve this dilemma by simply saying that everyone is at least a potential small group leader. Don't disqualify someone based on who they are or what they do within the church body.

It's also been said that unlikely people make good small group leaders. I agree. But I would also say likely people can also make good small group leaders.

My point is that since small groups are a basic expression of the church, most Christ-followers should at least be considered candidates for small group leadership.

❷ *We raise up*: "They must first be tested; and then if there is nothing against them, let them serve as deacons" (1 Timothy 3:10). We identify people who might be leaders, give them a chance to serve, and then appoint them to a place of leadership.

❸ *They rise up*: "Brothers, choose seven men from among you who are known to be full of the Spirit and wisdom. We will turn this responsibility over to them and will give our attention to prayer and the ministry of the word" (Acts 6:3, 4). People in the church who have gifts and abilities will naturally rise up and be recognized as leaders.

LEADERS NEED COMMUNITY VALUES

Research and experience have shown time and again that no one gift mix, personality type, or knowledge level qualifies a person to be a group leader. The essential element to becoming a faith-oriented small group leader is the person's heart. A small group leader must love God and love group members. One of the important keys to being an outstanding leader of a small group is exhibiting a servant's heart—a passion for those the Lord has brought around you and your leadership team. So how can you create that kind of passion in the relationships in your small group? This passion is driven by values.

CONSIDER THIS...

People will not put their hearts into things they don't believe in. In fact, people tend to show great commitment to the things they believe in most. When selecting group leaders, ask yourself questions like:

Here is a very important truth: clarity of values is the energy that makes the difference in a group member's commitment to the group. If your group members do not know your heart and passions as a leader, they may be unwilling to perform the tasks that all groups need to be successful and effective. They may exhibit sporadic attendance patterns. They may not do the right things outside of group or show up to group on time. But research has shown that when a leader defines group values and creates an understanding of the values with others in the group, participants feel a sense of commitment to the group and the leader! Value-setting is more than transparent living, though that is an essential element. By setting values the leader understands the important role he or she plays in establishing an atmosphere where the heart of a leader and a group can grow together!

—Source: Jon Weiner, SmallGroups.com

✦ What motivates this potential group leader?

✦ Are potential group members important to this leader?

✦ Will potential group members find this leader's heart credible?

✦ Is the potential group leader's character and values compatible with the value of Christian community in the church's small group ministry?

LEADERS NEED TRAINING AND ONGOING SUPPORT

Once you have selected small group leaders, determine your training strategy. Most churches who have been doing small group ministry for any time say that training is always a moving target, meaning that training tactics may need to be changed and fine-tuned often to make training most effective.

More Help!

To help leaders develop the heart necessary to lead, buy each a copy of the Small Group HELP! Guide, Who Me...A Leader? by Michael Mack. This book looks at six heart attributes of Jesus as he led his small group and helps leaders develop the same heart.

CONFESSIONS OF A SMALL GROUP DIRECTOR

It was just over a year ago that I came to this church as small groups minister. One of our core values is that life change happens best in small groups. Yet, without a staff person giving full-time attention to small groups for several years, the opportunities for long-term success were minimal and the possibility for problems was optimal.

Over the past year, several small groups have stopped meeting. No particular reason was given; just a lack of interest, I guess you could say. Because of a weak system of oversight and support, we did not learn of some groups' demise until months after the fact. Many small groups had issues and problems that the leaders had no idea how to deal with. So the groups disintegrated. In a couple groups, the leaders lost interest and terminated the groups. They had been "recruited" at one time to lead a small group but never really had a passion—or been impassioned—for it. One group dealt with major issues—a divorce among one couple in the group and individuals who turned away from God. The group first drifted apart and then broke apart. I believe the members are still hurting. Another group ended literally in a cursing session between some of the participants.

It's really no secret why these groups failed. It all comes down to a lack of leadership training and support.

Many of the leaders had been asked to lead a group, given a curriculum, and sent on their way. The leaders were never really envisioned or equipped for what they were being asked to do. The most training many of them received was a brief class on the basics of leading a group. The church had a coaching system in place, but the coaches were no better prepared for their important role. Many, I found out, had been recruited, handed Willow Creek's Coaching Manual, given five leaders, and sent out to do whatever they thought coaching meant. I learned after my arrival that coaching meant widely different things to different coaches.

As I talk with church leaders involved in small groups across the country, it seems to me that our church is a good example of what is going on—or not going on—in many churches. Worse yet, I fear, the urgency to get people connected in some large churches has stimulated a new fad in small group circles of starting up small groups with no or very little training.

—Source: Michael Mack, SmallGroups.com

Jesus spent three years with his disciples before releasing them to lead on their own. His leadership training could be described by words such as intentional, intense, practical, modeling, hands-on, encouraging, and transformational. Throughout the New Testament church, Jesus' pattern of discipleship was replicated. Without intentional, up-front leadership training, many questions arise:

> **REMEMBER: Training tactics may need to be changed and fine-tuned often to make training most effective.**

➤ *When a group member asks a doctrinal question, does the leader answer off the top of his head from a teaching she heard on a radio program? from his own opinion on the matter? or from Scripture?* **My experience, unfortunately, is that the poorly trained leader usually talks off the top of his head. Train your leaders how to help their groups discover the answers for themselves in Scripture.**

➤ *How can we know the hearts of small group leaders?* **Without spending much time with them in advance, all we can see is the way man sees them—from the outward** appearances of skills, knowledge, and charisma. Spend time with group leaders to see what God sees—their hearts.

➤ *How can we know the character and integrity of leaders: in their marriages, workplaces, and neighborhoods?* Group leaders do not have to be perfect, but they are a model of Christ-like living. How can we ascertain that without spending time with them?

➤ *How can we know for sure if they understand the vision and values of our small group ministries?* If they do not, they can easily steer their groups off-course from the mission, vision, and purposes of the church.

➤ *How can we equip them with the necessary skills to shepherd a small flock of God's people?* Without some upfront training, how can a leader know how to deal with difficulties? Where will they develop the skills of listening, asking follow-up questions, and sharing leadership?

➤ *How can we assure that they are leading people toward God and spiritual maturity, rather than in some other direction?*

➤ *How can we develop people in small groups who will grow and eventually be sent to start new groups?*

CASE STUDY

How a Church Launched a Small Group Ministry

(Source: SmallGroups.com)

Today, a leadership training track is in place at our church. Up-front training involves two modules: (1) a three-hour "Basic Training" workshop and (2) an apprenticeship. A potential leader has three options for the apprenticeship:

➤ Serve as an apprentice under a current leader in an existing small group

➤ Be involved in a three to four month Turbo Group (a group in which all members are apprentices, who later disband to lead other groups)

➤ Experienced leaders (who have led groups in other ministries in our church or have led a small group in another church) can start a group with a Small Group Mentor (one of our more experienced leaders) who provides one-on-one coaching for the first three months of the group. This coaching is more intense at first and scales back over time.

It may seem like using intentional, intense training would limit the numbers of small groups we can start. But that is not true, particularly over the long-term. I could start 50 small groups in our church using untrained leaders. That would help us connect 500 people into a small group. Not bad. But how many of those groups will be alive one year from now? How many people will still be connected in community? How many of them will have grown in their faith? How many will grow to the point of being prepared to lead others (see Hebrews 5:11–6:1)?

On the other hand, if I can start one small group today and send out just ten well-equipped leaders in six months, I know the people in those groups will be connected in community and to Christ, they will be in a much better position to grow spiritually, and they will more likely grow to the point of being sent to help start another small group. As each of those groups send out well-equipped leaders, the multiplication continues, so that many more than 500 people can be connected. And not just connected in a group, but connected in transformational community that will continue to send.

—Source: Michael Mack, SmallGroups.com

Look for the best tools to help train your leaders!

A survey on SmallGroups.com identified the eight training tools most frequently used as part of a small group leader's training path. Following is the list in alphabetical order.

1 **Apprenticing (on-the-job experience).** There is little that can replace the experience of actually watching someone lead a group from within and following Jesus' discipleship model:

1. I do; you watch
2. I do; you assist
3. You do; I assist
4. You do; I watch

2 **Books.** The Internet has revolutionized book selection and buying. No longer must you wonder whether a particular book will be helpful to your ministry or not. An abundance of book reviews can now be found online. Many online bookstores also include sample portions of books as well as reader reviews, so you can try before you buy. Sometimes you can get "advance looks" in the form of e-books or portions of new books before they are released.

3 **Curriculum Study Guides (and Leader Guides).** Many small group curriculum study guides have built-in leader guides (in the guide itself, on DVDs, or online) to help you facilitate the study as well as develop your group leadership skills.

4 **In-house Training Events.** Gathering small group leaders together for instruction is a great way to communicate a uniform message and inspire with vision and testimonies. The challenge, many small group ministry leaders say, is getting leaders to come to training events. Scheduling, frequency, and promotion are keys to making in-house events work.

5 **E-mail.** E-mail is used for everything from personal one-on-one communication to mass-distributed e-mail newsletters going to thousands.

6 **Outside (off-site) Training Events.** The Internet is a great place to find information on training events. Check out a current list on the SmallGroups.com "Training Calendar." Beyond listings of training events, you can often find online reviews of training events and magazine ads that will help you choose the best training event for your small group leadership team to attend together.

7   **Personal Coaching.** Coaching, like apprenticing, is a relational task that traditionally happens face-to-face. A more experienced small group leader helps a less experienced small group leader.

8   **Web Sites.** The Internet is an incredible small group information source. However, just because you know a great Web site does not mean that your small group leaders will know how to browse around the site as easily as you do. If you send a link to a Web site for your leaders to check out, be specific. Send all the important information like login procedures and specific page addresses you want them to view. If possible, hyperlink right from the document or e-mail. It also helps to have a short list of sites that you check regularly. This helps you cut down on your Internet search times and find the nuggets of information that will be most useful to your ministry situation.

SMALL GROUP LEADER ROLES

While the role of the small group leader should be simple, you may think about it in many different ways. Depending on how small groups are positioned in your church, you might use any of the following descriptions as a framework for developing a job description for your potential small group leader: Friend, Shepherd, Spiritual Director, Teacher, Ministry Team Leader, Mentor to Apprentices, Facilitator, Lay Pastor.

As you develop the job description for small group leaders, keep in mind that leaders tend to be people who are already busy. Build into your job description the requirement for rest and refreshment. You can help your small group leaders stay energized by teaching them to manage their "span of care."

Span of care is the number of people, activities, and projects for which you have significant responsibility. While small group leaders may be involved

TOP 10

SIGNS THE LEADER HAS LOST CONTROL OF A MEETING

10. After the opening worship and prayer time, your apprentice puts in a movie to watch.

9. The furloughed missionary you invited to your group to give a five-minute update from the field is saying, "God has really laid it on my heart to share with you a challenge from 2 Corinthians 7-9. I call this message 'The Ten Principles of Giving.'"

8. Two members are fist fighting over who's going to open the meeting in prayer.

7. The group has disintegrated into two camps who are chanting angrily at each other: "Regular!" "Decaf!" "Regular!" "Decaf!"

6. Members gaze into their crystals before answering any questions.

5. Members can't stop laughing at the host couple's friendly, frisky pooch that has a real affection for your right leg.

4. Members begin singing "Free Bird."

3. Group members ignore your plea of "How 'bout we get started?" and continue arguing over whether to watch the Home Shopping Network or Monday Night Football.

2. After prayer time you open your eyes to find everyone in the kitchen eating again.

1. Members start doing the Macarena to the Twila Paris CD you've got playing in the background.

(Source: SmallGroups.com)

in many ministry activities that are very worthy of their attention, each of these responsibilities compete for their available time, energy, and emotional resources. The risk involved in exceeding their healthy span of care is that they may lose their ability to effectively respond to the care and development needs of those they shepherd in their small group.

Studies show that on average people have twelve individuals in their lives whose death or loss of connection would be devastating to them. So to maintain emotional stability, the most we are typically able to care for and invest ourselves deeply in at any one time is twelve people. When you consider your immediate family is part of that twelve, then the number you can effectively shepherd in a small group is probably considerably less than that.

If your healthy span of care—either activities or people—exceeds your ability, then competition for your time and energy can render you ineffective. You can feel incredibly productive and have contact in many people's lives, yet not be able to shepherd those who have been entrusted to your care. Worse yet, constantly exceeding your span of care will drain your energy and emotions to the point of burnout. This is a human reality, but it is a reality that is particularly relevant to small group leaders. The condition of burnout and a desperate need for rest is alive and well among many small group leaders because of constant violation of healthy spans of care.

As a small group leader, Jesus clearly modeled the need for healthy spans of care in his ministry. Not surprisingly, he chose a group of twelve for his primary development ministry. The Gospels go on to record that Jesus had an even more intense connection with only three of the twelve disciples.

There are many other places in Scripture that model appropriate and healthy spans of care, including Jethro's advice to Moses in Exodus 18, which advocated healthy span-of-care ratios of 1:5 and 1:10.

IT IS STILL ABOUT RELATIONSHIPS

As you start selecting and training small group leaders, remember leadership development still hinges on relationships. Think about your small group vision for the future and as a small group director, consider what it would be like to receive the following e-mail:

Dear Emma,

Today marks my second anniversary as a small group leader. I'd like to take this opportunity to thank you for supporting me all the way. During our last huddle, you asked us what our needs were and you said that our answers would help you a lot. I've been thinking about this for the past two weeks, and I'd like to share my thoughts with you.

As a young leader, sometimes I really do not know what I truly need. Yes, I have the passion and desire to serve God and others, but I don't really know how to get there. Frankly, when I first learned about the role of small group leader, I felt quite overwhelmed. Yes, I was excited about the ministry, but me—a shepherd leader? Me—helping others grow? Wow, that's very scary! My initial response was that I need to grow a lot more before I could handle this role. You assured me that in every ministry there is always the need to take the step of faith, and you assured me that the Holy Spirit is there to help me and guide me!

Now, as I look back at these two years of ministry, you are right! Yes, the Holy Spirit was indeed there to help me, and despite some bumps along the way, I can say I was stretched by him in many ways. I am closer to him than before. Throughout these two years, I see three things that were crucial to my development:

1. Vision. *Your team has set a strong vision for us to follow. Through the training courses, annual rallies, and monthly huddles, I now understand:*

- *The purpose of the ministry (why we are doing it)*
- *The goals of the ministry (where we are heading)*
- *The core values of the ministry (how we do it)*
- *My role as a small group leader (how I participate)*

I know that in the beginning my focus was mostly on myself. (How did I fare this time? I should have done this. I should have done that.) and my members (their prayer requests). But you've gradually encouraged me to divert our attention from just ourselves to the needs of the community and the world. Yes, it is more exciting to look at the world through God's eyes, and I now dare say that we are designed to be together to serve those around us who are hurting and in need.

Because the purpose of the ministry is so strong and the goals and core values so clearly defined, it has become part of our church's small group culture, which makes it much easier for us to implement the curriculum and develop our group into a community that advocates life transformation. I appreciate the fact that within this grand scheme of our church's vision (which can still be overwhelming to me at times), I have always been given the next small steps to accomplish. So, suddenly, the vision doesn't seem too overpowering, because I know that as long as we take it one step at a time, somehow, with God's grace, we will get there!

2. Equipping. *I am so thankful for all the training your team has provided me. The small group leader training course provided both skills training and character development. I benefited from the course tremendously. I especially enjoyed the part when we shared with one another our successes and failures. It made us feel good because we were relieved to know that those kind of issues don't just happen in our group, and we're there as a team to support one another as we go through them.*

The various resources (books, Web sites, reading materials, conference information) you gave us were very helpful. I would not know where to get them otherwise. Thanks for pointing us to those resources. It saved me a lot of time searching for them.

Speaking about time, this is really a scarce commodity within the life of a small group leader. It's not just the meetings we lead, it's the huddles, rallies, and trainings we have to attend. Please don't get me wrong; these are great training venues for me. It's just that apart from all these meetings, we still have many other church activities and programs to attend: prayer meetings, Sunday school, missions conference, visitations. This is why I truly appreciate your team's effort to teach us about rest and give groups permission to take time off as needed. I am grateful that the rest is taken in the context of taking a step back from our busy schedules to make room to listen to the still voice of our Lord. It has been truly a renewing experience for many of us.

3. Spiritual Companionship. Most important of all, I am very thankful that I not only have a coach but a spiritual companion. Thank you for treating me not just as a task or someone to fulfill the ministry's goals. I appreciate your seeing me as a human being— someone in the midst of family needs, career demands, and financial pressures—struggling to do my best for the Lord. I appreciate the fact that every time you meet with me, you always ask about my children and my job situation. I know that you pray regularly for me. This is why when I was on the verge of being laid off, you were the first one I called to seek prayer support.

Thank you for keeping me accountable. Although sometimes I feel the pressure, I do appreciate the fact that you constantly ask me about my walk with God. In fact, no one (not even the pastors) checks on me regularly to see if I've read the Word lately. I remembered once admitting to you that I hadn't touched the Bible for a month, and rather than condemning me, you challenged me to read the Gospel of Mark together with you. Every week for the next month, you called *me and shared encouraging words from the Scripture passages. I really felt that you were a friend who was willing to wait for me and help me during my struggling times on this spiritual journey. This weekly call meant a lot to me, and I was attracted by your desire to read and obey God's Word. I have learned a lot through this experience of reading the Word with you. Since then, whenever I have had group members that share with me that they're downcast and do not feel like reading the Word, I do the same to help them by challenging them to read the Word together and calling them weekly to encourage them.*

Emma, thank you for always believing in me and trusting that I am still a vessel in the process of being formed. Yes, God is not done with me yet, and I know that he will bring the best out of me. Thank you for being my friend!

Blessings! Jane

Now that you have a good handle on the vital role of small group leaders, you're ready to consider what your small groups will do.

What Do Your Small Groups Do?

At this point in the process, you have some values, perhaps some initial strategies and tactics to get small groups started. You have selected or identified leaders. You may have even established a time frame for when small groups will start meeting. Now the question arises, what will these groups do when they get together?

From my experience, when small group directors first start small groups, many tend to give their leaders some basic training on group dynamics, hand them prepared curriculum, and then "let go and let Christian community happen." While in the short term this strategy might work, in the longer term you have to be more intentional about incorporating your church values into the small group process.

The big question may be: What will your small groups do when they get together?

In This Chapter...

- Small group gatherings and the values of the church
- Small group curricula and agendas
- How leaders choose what to do next
- Passing on the right values
- How to be flexible and still have a longer-term plan

This is the best time, regardless of what types of small groups you have, to train and model for your leaders how small groups should live out the values you have selected.

CONFESSIONS OF A SMALL GROUP DIRECTOR

Leading a small group ministry requires a tricky balance. On one hand, you don't want to set the leadership skill bar too high for new leaders and make leading small groups appear to be at the level of rocket science. On the other hand, you don't want to set the leadership skill bar so low that leaders think there is absolutely nothing they need to do to be an effective group leader except read from a curriculum or play a DVD.

What type of expectations should church leaders have of small group leaders in how they lead their group? I have worked hard at helping group leaders know how to use the curriculum I gave them, but one of the mistakes I made was not helping them incorporate the values of Christian community into their group meetings.

We started several groups that met for the purpose of discussing the week's sermon from our Sunday worship service. Each group leader was supplied a complete outline of the sermon along with a detailed curriculum to be followed during group meetings. Hardly any preparation was required for the leader or the group except having heard the sermon from the previous week. After a few months, several group leaders told us about needs in their groups that a discussion on the Sunday sermon was not meeting. After some discussion at the leadership level, we decided that these small groups could have freedom to choose their own study focus.

Once groups were released from following the Sunday teaching curriculum format, groups chose their own study focus, but a majority of these groups disbanded within six months.

We realized afterward the problem was that groups only knew how to do group life together in the context of the pastor's sermon curriculum we handed out every week. We never trained our leaders how to facilitate the values of the church, which were fellowship, discipleship, outreach, worship, and service. We never trained people how to do ministry in each of these value areas in the context of loving, multiplying relationships. If we had, as we learned later, we could have built sustainable reproducing groups whose existence would not have hinged on the curriculum we were supplying.

—Source: D. L., SmallGroups.com

One of the goals for your groups' gatherings is for them to model what life in Christ looks like, and in turn, what the church should look like. And you want that model to be highly reproducible. When you don't ground your small groups with core practices and expectations, they will tend to lose their focus once the excitement of the initial study wears off or the initial time commitment for the group to meet runs out.

GROUP AGENDAS AND CURRICULUM

One of the secrets of effective small group ministry is to train group leaders to think in terms of developing a group agenda rather than relying exclusively on a curriculum. Specifically, train leaders to develop a small group agenda that incorporates all the values you have adopted for your ministry. Curriculum is simply a tool that is part of the group agenda.

Benefits of a Group Agenda

Mike Shepherd suggests these ten benefits for group leaders using an agenda to lead their groups.

Definitions

Agenda: A list or program of things to be done or considered —Source: Dictionary.com *For a Christian small group, an agenda is a way to turn your values into activities that your group can do.*

1. *You become good stewards of your group member's time. Time is the commodity of our days.*

2. *A good agenda facilitates community development.*

3. *Individual sharing moves from low-risk (icebreaker, relational Bible study questions) to high-risk (care time) sharing.*

4. *Group members become comfortable when they know there is a plan to follow.*

5. *You accomplish your objectives: to laugh together, interact with biblical truth, connect at a soul-deep level, and reach out and serve beyond the group.*

6. *You stay balanced with regard to touching people's minds, souls, and emotions.*

7. *Other member's gifts can be used in the meeting instead of one leader doing everything.*

8. *By using it regularly, group members learn the value of an agenda that they can then champion when they start new groups.*

9. *Seekers who come as guests are less threatened.*

10. *Everyone knows when the group meeting starts and ends.*

—Source: SmallGroups.com

AN EXAMPLE OF A SMALL GROUP AGENDA

Here's a basic example of a group agenda used for years by Lyman Coleman, founder of Serendipity. It is simple, but it works.

Gather the People: 10–60 minutes

- Use an icebreaker to create a fun connection.

- Facilitate group members bringing refreshments or a meal.

- Provide important group information about upcoming parties or events.

Caution

Never forget that a small group is part of a larger mission than just getting together or filling their heads with more information. The responsibility of an effective group leader is to facilitate discipleship and life change in people's lives. That is the bottom line. The group leader should think strategically about how that will happen. With regard to meetings, group leaders are the managers of the clock. An agenda provides invaluable benefits for the group leader to accomplish the divine objective.

—Source: Mike Shepherd, SmallGroups.com

- Have a transition activity to turn hearts from the world to the Lord, such as worship.

Bible Study or Group Task: 30–45 minutes

- Allow people to be as hands-on and relational as possible; involve everyone.

- If your group is service- or task-oriented, have a plan for accomplishing that task.

- Use relational and interactive questions that focus on application.
- Use personal examples.
- Make one or two practical applications to life.

Caring Time: 15–30 minutes

- Tie the lesson application or the task to a specific prayer focus.
- Consider using a prayer/praise handout.
- Cast vision for outreach or to fill the "empty chair" in the group circle.
- Provide time for prayer. (Subgroups of four or same-gender partners work great.)
- Make plans for how you will continue interacting through the week until you meet again.

More Help!

To help your leaders facilitate dynamic, life-changing discussions, be sure they read the Small Groups HELP! Guide, *Now That's a Good Question!* by Terry Powell.

Definitions

Empty Chair: A group always keeps one chair open to remind participants that the group is open to welcoming new people at every meeting. They talk about and pray for the person who will fill the open chair often.

The basic small group agenda may vary depending on the values of your ministry and the types of small groups you have, but remember that what happens in the small group time and in between small group gatherings will determine people's perception of small group life. Make that perception the correct one right off the bat. It is much easier to model the correct Christian community lifestyle initially than to correct a bad experience later.

WHEN YOU'RE TAKING TME TO PLAN FOR YOUR SMALL GROUP MEETING, REMEMBER TO PLAN HOW YOU'LL CONTINUE INTERACTING UNTIL YOU MEET AGAIN.

Some curricula are better than others at providing components of a balanced agenda. But the key is getting your agenda focused around all aspects of Christian community and not relying on a single curriculum to do that for you.

"One Another" Agendas

A key question is: How well does your agenda or your curriculum choices over time reinforce and apply the "one another" commands found in the New Testament? These commands include:

TOP 10

THINGS THE APOSTLE PAUL WOULD SAY ABOUT SMALL GROUP GATHERINGS

10. "Eat, eat, eat! Haven't you folks ever heard of fasting?"

9. "That's not at all what I meant!"

8. "My dear friends, I am writing to you today to tell you that Twizzlers and Yahoo are not acceptable refreshments."

7. "Anyone want to see slides from my last mission trip?"

6. "Let all things in your group be done decently and in order. If anyone asks a discussion question, let there be only two or at most three responses, and each in turn; and then, let's move on to the next question."

5. "One of you says, 'I follow Paul,' another 'I follow Apollos,' another 'I follow Bill Hybels,' still another 'I only read Max Lucado.'"

4. "What shall we say then? Shall we continue this video series until all are sleeping? May it never be!"

3. "Harold, you can stop greeting Heather with a holy kiss now. Harold…Harold!"

2. "For what I received I passed on to you as of first importance: without a good child care policy, your group will fail."

1. "I plead with Euodia and I plead with Syntyche to agree with each other on who's bringing dessert next meeting."

(Source: SmallGroups.com)

➡ *"Encourage one another daily"* (Hebrews 3:13).

➡ *"Build each other up"* (1 Thessalonians 5:11).

➡ *"Spur one another on toward love and good deeds"* (Hebrews 10:24).

➡ *"Confess your sins to each other"* (James 5:16).

➡ *"Accept one another, then, just as Christ accepted you"* (Romans 15:7).

➡ *"Admonish one another"* (Colossians 3:16).

➡ *"Love one another deeply, from the heart"* (1 Peter 1:22).

Most biblical community commands will never be obeyed while groups have their noses in study guide books. Small groups have to be intentional about incorporating activities that promote obedience to these commands. Curricula can encourage and teach participants to be obedient to these commands, but if groups are just picking and choosing curricula without a plan, they will likely miss many opportunities to live in real Christian community. However, if groups develop an agenda strategy that takes your church values and the "one anothers" into consideration, then over time the groups will be more effective at incorporating all these principles into small group life.

CHOOSING A GROUP FOCUS

One of the questions often heard in small groups is, "What are we going to study next?" That question shows a lack of direction and a lack of real leadership. Rather than sailing toward a destination, many small groups are like a sailboat at sea being *tossed back and forth by the waves, and blown here and there by every wind of teaching"* (Ephesians 4:14).

WiSe WoRds

"As the basic building blocks of Christian fellowship, [the "one another" passages in Scripture] characterize the ways we should relate to one another within the body of Christ."

—Richard C. Meyer, *One Anothering*

Small group leaders should be asking at least four other questions, says Michael Mack. Teach your leaders to ask the right questions and follow the right principles to choose the right study:

✔ **QUESTION #1: Why does the group exist?**

✔ **PRINCIPLE: The main purpose of every group should flow out of the mission of the church.**

The mission of the church where I lead is, "To team with God in turning unchurched people into fully devoted followers of Jesus Christ." Your church's mission statement is probably similar in that it relates to carrying out the commission Jesus gave his church (Matthew 28:19, 20).

Once you have clarified your group's mission, writing it down if you have not done so already, you then need to answer the question, "What can we study that will help us carry out that mission? What should we study that will help us make disciples of Jesus?"

✔ QUESTION #2: Who is in my group?

✔ PRINCIPLE: The small group leader's main function is that of a shepherd who knows his sheep.

Here are several more questions the group leader should answer to help shepherd his group.

• *Where are members spiritually? As a shepherd, you must know where people are individually and where the group is as a whole. Are participants newborns in the faith, like spiritual teenagers, or are they mature adults? (See passages such as 1 John 2:12-14; 1 Peter 2:2; 1 Corinthians 3:1-3; and Hebrews 5:11-6:1 for discussions on how to shepherd people at different spiritual levels.)*

• *In what areas do they need to grow? Do they need more knowledge about beliefs and doctrine? Have they learned the disciplines of the Christian life? Are they familiar with the virtues of the Christian life or the fruit of the Spirit?*

• *How do they learn best? Do participants in your group tend to learn best through application-oriented discussion, by doing, hearing, reading, or a combination? Would individuals learn better in the group setting, or would some one-on-one mentoring be helpful?*

✔ QUESTION #3: What do you believe?

✔ PRINCIPLE: "Teach what is in accord with sound doctrine" (Titus 2:1).

As you choose curriculum, be sure it leads you to study God's Word, not just someone's opinions, even opinions that relate to Scripture. Satan is sneaky. He can, without a group even realizing it, knock you off track through innocent-sounding questions. Be careful! A writer can easily move a group to consider his opinions about a doctrinal stance by asking a series of questions that lead the conversation in a certain direction. Examine a Bible study closely before using it in your group. If you don't feel confident or competent to examine a curriculum piece for doctrinal purity, ask a church leader to do so first. Some churches have an "approved" list of studies that have already been reviewed. Know what your church teaches on certain "gray areas" of doctrinal issues.

✔ **QUESTION #4: What are your group's capabilities and limitations?**

✔ **PRINCIPLE: A small group agreement (covenant) can help establish some basic ground rules for Bible study selection.**

Some considerations:

- *Depth of studies.* Are the studies too deep? not deep enough? just right for your group?

- *Homework.* Has your group agreed to do "homework" between studies? Doing some in preparation for the next study can be a good approach for deep discipleship, but it also can tend to close a group, since no one wants to come to a group and be the only ones not to have the assignment done. If you do choose to use studies that include some homework, how much is appropriate? Talk about these questions before looking for a study.

- *Length of study.* How many weeks will the study take? Know the attention span of your group! Most groups get antsy with more than a six- or seven-week study. The old standby of thirteen-week studies does not usually work anymore. Shorter seems better, but discuss this with your group first.

- *Length of time in each study.* How much time will you spend in Bible study in each session? Are there too many questions for the time allotted by the group? Will projects take too long to complete?

- *Good questions.* Will the questions in the study lead to discussion and lively interaction, or do the questions sound like a pop quiz, looking for one-sentence answers? Also consider how many questions is enough for a good discussion. Some Bible studies include fifteen or more questions. That may be way too many for most groups, unless you are expecting one person to answer each question. But that is not a discussion! Sometimes two or three good application-oriented questions are enough for a stimulating, interactive, life-changing discussion around God's Word.

• *Open or closed.* A long study or series may inadvertently close your group. New people feel awkward jumping into the middle of a study— they feel like they are behind even before they start! Do sessions build upon each other or are they somewhat independent, so that new people can easily join at any time?

• *Cost.* This may be the biggie! Discuss with your group how much members want to shell out for Bible-study guides. The price of some curriculum choices may be prohibitive for some participants' budgets. Be sensitive to this. Be a good steward of the resources God has provided.

• *Your own limitations.* What are you capable of preparing given your schedule? What studies would work best for your level of Bible knowledge and abilities? Would a DVD series be better, since it usually includes some good teaching? What are you competent to do based on your giftedness? This is where your group can help. Lean on people who have the time and giftedness to do the things you cannot.

Help group leaders answer these questions and follow these principles so they can navigate the sea of curriculum choices successfully. Better yet, enable them to lead their groups to the destination God desires for them so you will never again hear someone ask, *"So…what do you think our small group should study next?"*

—Source: SmallGroups.com

WARNING: SMALL GROUP MEETINGS DON'T ALWAYS HAPPEN THE WAY THE AGENDA SAYS THEY SHOULD!

A small group leader can have the best long-term plan and run the mechanics of the small group agenda with skill and still not have a life-changing

small group. Regardless of the type of a small group, the overriding purpose is for Christian community to be life changing.

Agendas don't change people's lives. Christ does. Group members' relationships with him and with one another are the environment in which life change can happen.

Terminal illness…divorce…parenting issues… financial stress…The list of human problems that will not be on a leader's meeting agenda seems endless. When thinking about the people who face these life struggles, one of the biggest jobs of a small group leader is not so much to be a teacher, as it is to be a navigator. As author Thom Bandy puts it, small group leaders are "midwives" who are constantly coaching the painful birth of something new that God is doing in group members' lives.

A leader's response to people's struggles is not necessarily, "Can I help you find a solution to this pain?" or "What knowledge or scriptural application do you lack that would make your situation better?" Rather it is, "Can I help this new thing to be born and to grow in you?"

TOP 10 WORST TOPICAL BIBLE STUDIES

10. Adam and Eve: Weaving Fig Leaves in a Frenzy

9. The Biblical Diet Plan: Fasting

8. Did Adam Have a Belly Button?

7. Polygamy: Men with Complicated Lives

6. Gossip: The Art of Sharing Prayer Requests Without Really Praying

5. Grief: Get Over It!

4. You Think You've Got It Bad? A Study of Jeremiah and Lamentations

3. How To Build a Fireproof Compound for Your Small Group

2. Methods of Death: Beheading and Being Run Through with a Sword

1. Winning at Lotto through Hidden Codes in Scripture

(Source: SmallGroups.com)

The key to helping group members navigate through chaotic life involves helping them process the love and truth of an infinite God, while dealing with any number of finite human problems. When people do not wrestle with that intersection, it leaves them feeling disconnected and makes the chaos seem as pronounced as ever.

Intersection Questions

These questions can help individuals find the intersection of the finite and infinite in such a way as to make sense of their current situation and to take courage for the future.

"Would you be open to discovering what the Bible says about your life in this circumstance?"

"Where has your story and God's story intersected recently?

"If you really believed the Word we have studied tonight, how would it change your life?"

"What is God saying to you right now?"

"How will you live differently tomorrow because of what we have talked about today?"

—Source: Tom Bandy, SmallGroups.com

Small group leaders can help bring some order to the chaos. At any given time and in any given situation, the Christian leader can help position group members in between the finite and the infinite. A leader can ask hurting group members some simple questions, such as the ones in the box, to help group members position themselves correctly.

HOW IN THE WORLD CAN GROUP LEADERS GET ALL OF THIS ACCOMPLISHED?

As you look over your small group values—things like fellowship, discipleship, service, and outreach, for instance—it is unlikely, even with the best agenda, that your leaders will get all of these accomplished in an hour and a half once a week. This is particularly true when individual needs of group members surface that require the group to postpone the agenda for the group meeting and rally around someone in need of God's special touch.

So, you need to develop and train leaders to think in terms of finding a rhythm to community where these things can be incorporated into group life over time.

For instance, let's say service is one of the core values on the small group agenda. Group members can certainly serve one another daily, but if a leader wants the group to practice this value, he needs to occasionally plan a service activity for the group to do together. That might not be practical at every group gathering, of course, so instead, he can plan a service project once every couple of months. Better yet, designate someone in the group with gifting in helps and administration to coordinate a service project on a regular basis.

If a leader doesn't plan ahead, then things fall off the radar screen and the group agenda doesn't get accomplished, values don't get instilled into group

More Help!

Facing challenging situations and challenging people is almost a given in small groups. Buy your leaders copies of the Small Group HELP! Guide, Why Didn't You Warn Me? by Pat Sikora. Pat will show your leaders how to deal with all the most common challenges groups face.

FROM L-O-N-G TO SHORT

Group study guides commonly used to contain material for twelve or more sessions. Recently the trend is toward studies with much shorter horizons—six sessions or shorter. Dwelling on the same topic for twelve weeks or more makes participants feel like they are stuck in a rut and sometimes distracts groups from other values for weeks at a time.

Leader adjustment: It is fine to dive into longer group studies, but realize that group leaders need to help people apply God's Word in real time. One idea may be for groups to step away from the study focus for a few weeks to address group members' questions or focus on doing a service project. Help groups change their focus from "doing an X-week study" to experiencing a week-by-week journey together, with Jesus as the leader and teacher.

—Source: SmallGroups.com

members, and small groups tend to lose focus, becoming ingrown and hard to sustain over the long haul.

And remember, Jesus is the real leader of every small group. Continuously encourage leaders to pray and rely fully on his Spirit at work in their groups as they do life together.

CASE STUDY

Avoiding Poorly Run Meetings

Have you ever participated in a group meeting that was poorly run? It can drive you nuts. I got stuck in one of those meetings recently when I went to evaluate a particular small group. It was fun but chaotic to say the least. When I arrived, no one greeted me or extended any kind of welcome. I sat down. No one interacted with me. I waited for the meeting to start. It did, about twenty minutes later than it was supposed to. There were no refreshments. The leader stood up and said, "Well, what do you guys want to do tonight? Anybody have any ideas?" I kid you not. I thought I was in small group hell. It was awful.

Group leaders absolutely must plan an agenda for every group meeting. We are part of an incredible mission—to make disciples. We do not meet just to meet. We have a purpose.

As small group leaders plan small group gatherings, they should first ask and answer a few questions:

➤ What is the purpose of our group? Is it tied to the Great Commission?

➤ What kind of group are we: covenant, seeker, support, task, or something else?

➤ Are we an open or closed group?

Regardless of how leaders answer these questions, every group should have a basic group agenda.

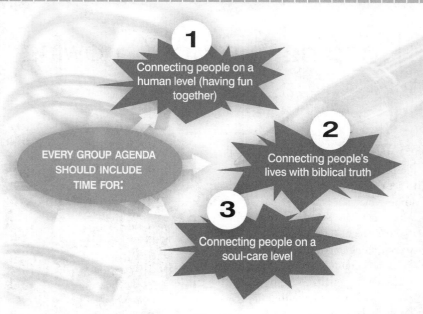

1
Connecting people on a human level (having fun together)

EVERY GROUP AGENDA SHOULD INCLUDE TIME FOR**:**

2
Connecting people's lives with biblical truth

3
Connecting people on a soul-care level

You can flesh that out in many different ways. For example, closed discipleship groups may include worship as a part of their meeting, while open seeker groups may not. Some groups may not have an actual Bible study every time they meet in order to interact with God's truth. They may study a book or watch a movie and evaluate its tenets in light of Scripture. The worst thing a group can do is the same thing at every meeting and not incorporate their basic values into the group process.

—Source: Mike Shepherd, SmallGroups.com

Once you get your small groups going, how do you keep them growing? I'll show you how in Chapter 5.

Keeping **5** Groups Growing

When churches start small group ministries, many have an initial strategy to get people into groups. However, that strategy may not continue to be effective as time goes on. Keeping groups growing is one of the big issues when it comes to continuing to grow the ministry of Christian community. One of the keys to sustained growth is keeping outreach a very high value and not to think of outreach too narrowly.

> ## In This Chapter...
> - Keep your focus on oneness rather than affinity.
> - Broaden your small group outreach scope.
> - Know how people get funneled into small groups.
> - Take your small groups to the people, rather than inviting people to your small groups.
> - Evaluate whether your small groups are open or closed.

STRIVING FOR AFFINITY OR ONENESS?

For years, small groups have formed around affinities: retirees, young parents, empty nesters, singles, sports groups, vocational groups, family status, hobbies, or personal interests. Affinities have proven to create the context that helps all types of groups form relationships and bond into a community. As a result, many churches tend to focus small group outreach strategies around affinity. But is the end goal to get small groups to bond around affinity or to realize oneness?

Consider Jesus' twelve disciples. When Jesus called them, what was his purpose

Definitions

Affinity: A natural attraction, liking, or feeling of kinship; relationship by alliance.

Oneness: Relationship characterized by unity of purpose and love even in the face of extreme opposition or internal conflict.

for this group? In John 17:11-21, Jesus prayed that the oneness of the disciples would be comparable to that of the Trinity. The result of that type of oneness is that the world will believe in Jesus.

In small groups, affinity, kinship, or even friendship is not the goal; they are only stepping-stones to something far more important: oneness.

Experience reveals and research confirms that group relationships and group bonds remain healthiest when a group keeps moving through the journey of discovering affinity, building oneness in community, and then embracing their mission to carry out the Great Commission as a direct result of their oneness. Affinity is only a stepping-stone along that journey.

WHO IS YOUR TARGET?

As you consider to whom your small groups will reach out, think in terms of two people groups:

❶ **The unconnected already in your church. These are the folks who already have some level of commitment to your larger church, either through your weekly worship services or another event.**

❷ **Those without any previous connection to your church. These are the non-Christians, the un-churched, the seekers in your community.**

A majority of small groups surveyed had at least one member who wasn't a regular attender of the church's weekly worship service.

Churches that have had the most success growing their small group ministries choose an outreach strategy that involves getting both church worship service attenders and the unchurched into small groups.

As far as the unchurched are concerned, a SmallGroups.com survey revealed that a majority of small groups surveyed already had at least one person in their group who wasn't a regular attender of the church's weekly worship service. This points to the reality that open, healthy small groups are proving themselves to be very effective "entry doors" to the church. In fact, they may be a preferred entry door for several reasons:

Relationships. Most studies say the key to retention is relationships. The likelihood of a visitor to worship services "sticking" correlates closely to whether the visitor makes meaningful connections with others in the congregation. In small group outreach, the likelihood of meaningful connections being made to others in the group is much higher due to the relational nature of group life.

Culture Change. Our postmodern culture is creating people who have become starved for meaningful relationships and significance. Small groups are a preferred environment where these relationships and meaningful service opportunities can happen.

Decentralized Resources. Worship-service visitor hospitality and follow-up require a great deal of planning and time and are typically done by only a few as part of a ministry team or committee assigned to this task. Small group outreach and follow-up is a ministry of the small group as a whole and becomes a natural part of the group's life together.

Accessibility for Any Church. Many churches who struggle to attract visitors through their weekend worship services (because of facility limitations or worship-style issues) may more easily implement a small group outreach strategy. Many would find it easier to train small group leaders to develop groups with an "outward focus" rather than to train an entire congregation to accept a new worship style designed to be "outwardly focused."

Reproducible. A highly programmed, high-quality worship service designed to appeal to new visitors requires specific gifts and resources not immediately available to every church. However, a small group functioning in community already has most of the outside relational connections and internal hospitality resources to make outreach doable and reproducible as groups grow and multiply.

FROM "DOORS" TO "FUNNELS"

If small groups are the entry door, think of the way you get people into the small group entry door as a "funnel." A funnel is a device that has a wide opening at one end and a small opening at the other. Funnels help get things into small, hard-to-access openings. Likewise, funnels help guide people into small groups.

Small groups often form and grow as people are drawn to do life together out of larger groups of people. How people get from the larger group to the smaller group is the "funnel" or the pathway used to bring people into community. Three different funnels are typically used in church small group ministries. The bottom line is that regardless of which funnel you use, the long-term results of your small group ministry will depend on the core values instilled as people travel through the funnel into small group communities.

The Silo Funnel

Every church has "small groups" whether they try to or not. Every church has relational clusters that exist in small Sunday school classes, choirs, or even what some people call "cliques."

One way to form small groups where spiritual development is a core value is to start with the relationships that already exist. All you have to do is add some intentionality to it: train a leader, recommend a meeting schedule, provide an agenda, and have a church leader draw a circle around them and call them a group!

Obviously, healthy disciple-making groups do not always self-initiate, so the Silo Funnel can help it happen. To help people embrace the new values of group life, many times a special catalytic event or campaign is used to help launch new groups. New groups can be established wherever existing relational connections can be identified, a leader-host can be established, and some basic training provided.

SILO FUNNEL

Small Sunday school class, worship team, ministry task groups, good friends, etc.

Small groups

CONFESSIONS OF A SMALL GROUP DIRECTOR

My observation has been that small groups that are formed through preexisting relational connections are very strong and sustainable for long periods of time. These groups can also have great discipleship potential as existing relationships flourish from the added injection of intentional Bible study, consistent and purposeful fellowship, service, and accountability. When these groups are continually engrained with strong values of outreach, service, and multiplication, they can become consistent disciple-making communities. However, my experience has been that these groups easily drift toward non-reproducibility and in the worst cases become unproductive holding tanks.

Good friends form a small group to do Bible study and service. The community is rich, and the group instinctively protects the safety of the environment by either subtly discouraging new members from joining or turning down new opportunities for mission that might disrupt group life. The result is that new people and ideas come and go, but the inner circle remains strong and resistant to change.

My experience has been that, by itself, the Silo Funnel can establish several stable groups, but many preexisting small groups and classes will never embrace the full vision and mission of the new small group ministry; instead they will remain "out of network," and in many cases, remain unfruitful. Thus only a relatively small percentage of the whole church becomes connected to an intentional small group focused on spiritual development. The groups that remain tend to have intrinsically low motivation for outreach and multiplication over time.

—Source: SmallGroups.com

The Fishing Pond Funnel

This strategy involves raising up and training small group leaders. These leaders then "fish" for their own group members in different "ponds" of people already connected to the larger church. The ponds consist of people-groups who have been drawn to the church through other activities like worship services. These ponds may include first-time worship-service visitors, new members, singles, sports ministries, or the infamous "those not in a group" list. Building and growing groups revolve around personal invitation with some help from church leadership to direct leaders toward the ponds.

FISHING POND FUNNEL

First-time worship service visitors, new members, those not in a group, men's ministry, women's ministry, special interests, etc.

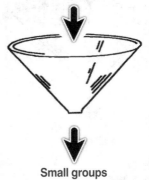

Small groups

The Fishing Pond Funnel works best in church situations where new people are consistently drawn to large group events like worship services and where there is a mechanism to continually raise up new leaders. In many cases, the bigger the pond, the easier it is to find both new leaders and potential group members. This funnel can lead many into groups and has the potential to capture new people in groups in an ongoing basis. The effectiveness of this funnel is really dependent on new leader development, ongoing leadership support, and the curriculum or "recipe" used to help the group through the phases of community development, since leaders and group members do not often have prior relational connections.

While the potential to connect a larger percentage of the congregation is increased with this funnel, I have found that these groups tend to be less sustainable because groups do not typically form around preexisting relationships or geography. Many times individual ministries of the church (men's, women's, greeters, music, youth, and so forth) develop their own way to funnel people into groups, which can lead to confusion of values and even competition. Also, leadership development and leader coaching is critically important, since many group leaders have had few previous small group experiences. Without leader support, many groups end prematurely, become less purposeful, or eventually become holding tanks rather than disciple-producers.

My experience is that the more you support and coach your leaders, the more effective group and leader multiplication tends to be, and the higher the percentage of the congregation that can potentially be involved in small groups when using the Fishing Pond Funnel.

—Source: SmallGroups.com

The Farm System Funnel

The first two strategies involve some centralized feeder system in which the larger church becomes the main feeder into the small groups. In the Farm System Funnel, groups develop their own feeder system with respect to outreach prospects. Each group's spiritual cultivation, seed sowing, and sometimes harvest is mostly decentralized from the larger congregation. The farm system focuses on establishing relationships and inviting people to their group from their spheres of influence: their families, schools, neighborhoods, or workplaces.

FARM SYSTEM FUNNEL

Neighbors, classmates, co-workers, family, friends, worship service attenders, etc.

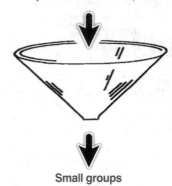

Small groups

CONFESSIONS OF A SMALL GROUP DIRECTOR

What makes this strategy work is the group's focus on developing relationships with those in their "neighborhoods" prior to inviting them to their group. This funnel will reach people the large-group gathering approach might never reach. However, the Farm System Funnel requires a different paradigm that allows individuals in the group to see outreach and service as their job and not "the church's job." Because of that difficult paradigm shift, the Farm System Funnel is less effective in church situations where established members have their whole relational network within the church congregation itself. Establishing relationships with unchurched people is time-intensive, and a heavy "church" activity calendar can actually be a barrier to establishing these relationships. Strong ongoing leadership support is also vitally important in this funnel.

My experience is that if the value of small group outreach beyond the "walls" of the congregation really takes hold, significantly more people will be in small groups than those who attend the large-group worship service. In fact, I have found that getting new small group members to attend large group worship services in a decentralized paradigm sometimes becomes as much of a challenge as getting large-group worship-service attenders to connect to small groups in a centralized paradigm.

—Source: SmallGroups.com

As you evaluate which funnel to use in your church, realize that you will likely have some of all three strategies (and more) in your church simultaneously. Depending on the size of your small group ministry, it may be strategic to use all three funnels. However, if you are establishing or transitioning a small group ministry, keep these two things in mind:

① SELECTING A FUNNEL

Make sure you and your leadership are as clear as possible on which funnel you are using to grow and reproduce your groups. Teach and demonstrate those values from the top down in your leader- ship structure. Also, select your funnel in the beginning with the end in mind. If you start small groups congregation-wide with the Silo-Funnel approach and then a year later want your groups to start reaching out to the neighborhoods where they meet, this will become a hard sell for most of your groups. Whichever funnel you choose, train your people to have a long-term vision and strategy for keeping groups healthy and growing. Otherwise, groups can become holding tanks rather than disciple-making vehicles.

The more restricted the large end of your funnel is, the more difficult it is to maintain group health and group growth over the long haul. A funnel with a narrow opening (Silo Funnel) can produce incredible small groups initially, but making sure these groups are embracing mission and multiplication can be a more difficult process. On the other hand, groups that are formed from the Farm-System Funnel tend to be less cohesive and stable initially, but with good relational leadership come to function as dynamic Christian communities and have values of outreach and multiplication more engrained in their DNA.

② CASTING A VISION

Casting the vision for your selected funnel is vital. Regardless of which funnel you use, what comes out of your funnel must be small groups that have the core values that can be sustained over the long haul. From my experience, the best way to do that is to select a funnel that has the widest opening. Leaving your funnel open to those outside the walls of the defined church, including your neighbors, coworkers, classmates, and others is critical to the mission and growth of your group members as Christ followers.

TAKING YOUR SMALL GROUPS TO THE PEOPLE

The secret to having growing groups does not involve getting more people to come to your groups. It's about taking your small groups to the people.

Even a brief review of the workings of the New Testament church reveals that the gospel was most life changing when encountered in everyday life. For instance, Paul went to where the lost people were. He did not water down the truth, but he made the message relevant to people in their context. He described the process as one in which people can "reach out for [God] and find him, though he is not far from each one of us" (Acts 17:27).

TOP 10

WORST SERVANT EVANGELISM PROJECTS FOR YOUR SMALL GROUP

10. Give away free onion cakes outside the supermarket

9. Rake leaves unannounced at CIA headquarters

8. Pizza party for patients in the cardiac unit

7. Job-skills training at the nursing home

6. Surprise the local librarians by putting all the books in alphabetical order

5. Ticket-scalping ministry at the local professional ballpark

4. The "You looked kinda hungry, so we thought we'd pass along the fruitcake we didn't want for Christmas" soup kitchen

3. Give those nice men in the ski masks a ride home from the bank

2. Invite neighbors in to watch the Jesus film on Super Bowl Sunday

1. Street corner teeth-brushing and flossing outreach

(Source: SmallGroups.com)

CASE STUDY

Small Group Outreach

In our church, we wrestled with how to apply outreach in our small group ministry. When casting the vision for small group outreach, we constantly encountered a tension. The tension was between the small group members' desire for group intimacy and the mandate for group outreach. On one hand, followers of Christ naturally long for a committed discipleship group where honest sharing and in-depth probing of the Word occurs and where Christian community runs deep. On the other hand, Christ-following group members also recognize the mandate we have for participating in the Great Commission (Matthew 28:18-20), knowing that the energy and awkwardness involved in loving new people is part of our calling.

The solution to this tension for us became know as the "O-Group Strategy." Imagine the members of your group arranged in a circle of intimate nurturing relationships with one another. Most of our traditional thought processes about group outreach center on how to bring more new people into the circle (figure 1).

But what if you change your way of thinking? Instead of focusing on getting people into the circle, focus on ways for group members to create small group bonds with the disconnected even before they visit a small group.

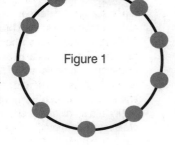

Figure 1

What if you defined success not by whether a new person showed up at the next group meeting, but by how you were faithfully investing your life in Christ on a regular basis with one or two others outside the group? What if you set up a schedule to have lunch with a non-believing coworker or disconnected church member twice a month just so you could get to know them? What if you shared a garden plot with your unchurched neighbor where you could routinely work together? What if you regularly carpooled to a child's or grandchild's sporting event with a new family at your church?

Then after you begin to develop that relationship and establish trust between you, suggest reading a book together about how to become a better parent from a biblical perspective. Or share a biblical teaching on CD or DVD and get their reaction to it the next time you get together.

Group members might apply this strategy with one or two or more people they would like to reach out to. Then, rather than defining success as bringing those people into the group circle, you define it as establishing connections to people outside of regular small group meetings. Now, a small group member has established a whole new group that we call an O-Group (Outreach Group). See figure 2:

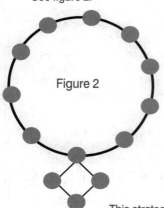

Figure 2

The O-Group is not isolated from the main group, because while these O-Group relationships are being established, you and your small group are praying for these O-Group individuals by name. Group members are also sharing with their O-Group people about what a great experience the regular small group is to them. They invite their O-Group people to share meals with other small group members occasionally. Pretty soon, every small group member has at least one person they are reaching out to, and the small group picture starts to look something like figure 3.

This strategy has made successful outreach attainable for everyone in our church. And that has created a whole new sense of enthusiasm about outreach. The obvious end result is that through prayer and relationships, O-Group people move easily into small group circles because over time other people from the group have also entered into a relationship with them. When the day comes for O-Group people to come to a regular group meeting, it's almost like they are regulars.

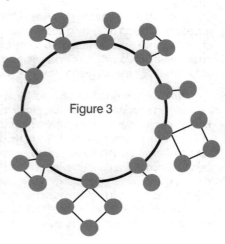

Figure 3

—Source: SmallGroups.com

OPEN VS. CLOSED SMALL GROUPS

So far in this chapter, we have been working on the assumption that your small groups are always open to new people. But some small group ministries have closed groups.

It may be appropriate for small groups to be closed for specific time periods. Groups that are focusing on regimented curricula or discipleship plans, recovery groups, support groups, and even leadership training groups can all be legitimately closed for a period of time. Even Jesus had a closed group for nearly three years.

However, in Jesus' group, periods of being closed were primarily growth and preparation times for new and expanded missions of outreach and service. In fact, Peter was exhorted at the Mount of Transfiguration (Luke 9:28-36) to not just build shrines of intimate experiences, but to move forward in obedience and mission.

The question repeatedly asked is: *"Can a group, whether a congregation or a small group, stay together, relatively intact, for long periods of time and maintain spiritual health and fruitfulness without new life and renewal being introduced? Can it really be 'us four and no more' forever?"* I have become more and more convinced over the years that a group that is well into its life cycle together can only sustain spiritual health and consistently experience seasons of renewal and rebirth by being open to new life coming into the group.

This new life can come in many forms: a new group member, a new group mission outside themselves, or the release of members to begin a new group or mission. To introduce God's new life, the group must be "open" at times.

> A NEW GROUP MEMBER

> A NEW GROUP MISSION OUTSIDE THEMSELVES

> THE RELEASE OF MEMBERS TO BEGIN A NEW GROUP

From a functional standpoint, groups that are not declared to be closed may, in fact, operate as a closed group after a time of relationship building. This is normal, but be aware of the drift in groups, especially where relational intimacy and relative comfort are the norm, and the trend is towards "ingrowth" and not outreach.

As Robert Lewis says in the Church of the Irresistible Influence, *"These groupings often end up as perpetual 'holding tanks' where Christians become increasingly comfortable with each other and themselves and increasingly disconnected from our world."* This leads to unhealthy consequences—needs soon turn to wants, a toxic self-absorption can easily develop, "us" becomes all that matters, and spiritual impact is rarely contemplated beyond the borders of the group.

They think the goal is harmony or serenity or good feelings, when in fact the goal is really mission, spiritual fruit, personal deepening, and the like.

The spiritual leader of the group needs to keep this correct focus and goal before the group and discern when to push the group toward openness and when to retreat into the safety of intimacy.

> **More Help**
> A valuable mechanism for openness is "The Blessing List" from Touch Outreach Ministries (The Cell Group People): *http://www. cellgrouppeople.com/.*

Keeping a group in a spiritually healthy balance of closed intimacy and open outreach requires Spirit-directed leadership and the incorporation of some essential practices. These practices include the following:

Openness must be declared in the covenant. Small group members must agree to and own the idea that the group's purpose at some point includes reaching out beyond themselves.

There must be a mechanism for openness. Whether it involves praying for the open chair, having an outreach list (prayer list or "Blessing List"), or scheduling an outreach service project, a tool or reminder of openness is critical.

Openness must be fostered through relationships, not programs. Programs for openness and outreach can be great tools, but until your group members value openness in their own hearts and in their relationships, little progress will be made.

An apprentice leader must be identified and developed. An apprentice is a constant reminder to the group of the eventual growth and multiplication of the group's mission of openness.

Leaders must model inviting people to the small group. It is likely the leader will be the first and most active person in inviting new people to the group. A group leader's call for group openness is not going to have much impact without also walking the talk.

A Long Push In the Same Direction

In This Chapter...

- If you can't easily reproduce the way you do ministry, then don't do it.
- Small group leaders need support from a leadership community.
- Small group leaders need relational coaches to help them be successful.
- All levels of the small group ministry should be evaluated for spiritual health.
- The Lord uses persistent servants; don't give up when it comes to Christian community.

As we have looked at ideas and principles for starting a small group ministry, our focus, as the book title suggests, is the start-up phase. The next question is, How do you keep all this going? Little thought is usually given to how you will keep a small group ministry growing in years two, three, four, five and beyond. But it is really important to think about that now. It is easy to put off this thought processing. It is important to start with the end in mind.

Keep in mind that relational ministry is not easy. It will require ongoing effort to build healthy Christian community. However, a few things will make the push easier as time goes on. That's the focus of this final chapter.

IF IT CAN'T BE REPRODUCED, DON'T DO IT

I believe in the heart of every committed Christ-follower is a desire to see God's kingdom grow and multiply. Most small group leaders whose groups have grown and who see many people still needing Christian community recognize the need to multiply leaders and groups. However, even while many churches recognize that small group multiplication is a good thing, the truth is:

Most churches do not have a philosophy of ministry that promotes small group multiplication.

Less than 5% of groups surveyed have plans to give birth to a new group or launch a new leader.

The longer small groups are together, the harder it is to assimilate new members and multiply new groups.

CONFESSIONS OF A SMALL GROUP DIRECTOR

SMALL GROUP MULTIPLICATION:

the process of reproducing biblical values, knowledge, experiences, and skills from one Christ-follower to another through relational and experiential processes. The process culminates when one small group leader releases another emerging small group leader to lead a new small group.

In school, children typically learn addition, and then subtraction, followed by multiplication and division. In spiritual life, I would argue it's more important to learn multiplication first, then addition, and avoid division and subtraction altogether.

Groups originating from either multiplication or addition can be very healthy and grow both in quality and quantity of people. But if they grow, they will eventually reach size and growth constraints. In these situations, some key decisions need to be made.

➤ *Do you leave those groups alone and praise them as a model of Christian community and then seek to add other leaders and small groups from outside the core of those existing groups to begin the process afresh (addition)?*

➤ *Or do you encourage the existing leaders and groups to replicate leaders and core members for new small groups (multiplication)?*

If you are the small group ministry point person at your church and the addition approach has been the default mode of operation, you need to know that introducing the concept of small group multiplication can create division within the group or division between the group and church leadership. I've been there, done that.

The problem is not that people are against the value of more people growing in their relationship in Christ. In fact, most can even understand how having two or more groups available could dramatically increase the capacity to add more people into this biblical community experience. It's just that they only learned to do that through addition—adding a new leader and core group members, but not from "their" group. That's why when they are faced with the prospect of the new group having "body donors" from their own group (multiplication), they feel like it's more about "dividing" and "subtracting" people from their existing group.

When I got involved with another church ministry, I started by teaching small group multiplication right off the bat, rather than starting with the addition philosophy. In that ministry, people accepted small group multiplication as normal—not easy, but normal.

Granted, just like in school, multiplication is a harder concept to master than addition, but in small group life, learning multiplication first makes it so much easier for small groups to reproduce themselves.

—Source: D. L., SmallGroups.com

If you are directing small group leaders, how do you help them learn to do multiplication, particularly if they have never gone through a multiplication process themselves? Here are a few lessons I've found helpful when teaching, training, and coaching small group leaders:

Lesson 1: Help leaders learn that small group multiplication reflects the biblical pattern.

How did church growth start in the New Testament? With Jesus and a handful of followers. Sure, large crowds were with Jesus at times, but there were only a handful of true followers. By pouring his life into a few, Jesus was able to reproduce much of his ministry into the first disciples—they relationally and experientially learned from Jesus how to multiply disciples.

Lesson 2: Learn that small group multiplication is typical in healthy churches.

In his landmark study, "Natural Church Development," Christian Schwartz conducted the largest church growth study ever, involving more than a thousand churches in thirty-two countries. Of the 170 variables in the study, one variable had more correlation to church growth than any other. Schwartz said, *"It is probably no coincidence that our computer survey selected the variable of 'holistic small groups: Our church consciously promotes the multiplication*

of small groups through cell division.' If we were to identify any one principle as the most important—even though our research shows that the interplay of all basic elements is important—then without a doubt it would be the multiplication of small groups."

TOP 10 — LAME EXCUSES FOR NOT MULTIPLYING (BIRTHING) A GROUP

10. We're looking for quality, not quantity.

9. Birthing? Isn't that painful?

8. "Multiply? Since we've started the outreach to expecting mothers, I feel like we multiply every week!"

7. There won't be "seconds" of Sandra's cherry cheesecake!

6. Doesn't that leave stretch marks?

5. I might have to give up my La-Z-Boy® for a cold, steel, fold-up chair.

4. We don't need to; we only have about twenty people coming to our group.

3. Visitors, Shmisitors.

2. My children are too young to explain the "birthing process."

1. Birthing is just not my gift.

(Source: SmallGroups.com)

Leaders are on the front lines as they lead their small groups into deeper experiences of community and discipleship.

SMALL GROUP LEADERS NEED COMMUNITY TOO

Do small group leaders have special needs for community that are not typically met in the small groups they lead? Can small group leaders lead and be sustained spiritually in relative isolation over long periods of time? Do experienced and spiritually mature leaders need more community than they are getting in their own small groups?

Leaders are on the front lines as they lead their small groups into deeper experiences of community and discipleship. If they don't have the opportunity to learn, be trained, and experience that community with other leaders and mentors, then it will be more difficult and at times discouraging to lead. Don't assume small group leaders can do all this without leadership community.

Where does that leadership community come from? It comes from relationships with other small group leaders. It comes from small group leaders and church leaders meeting together for training and support. It comes from leaders of leaders who help guide less experienced small group leaders along the way. These leaders of leaders have been called many things: shepherds, pastors, area leaders, or small group leader coaches.

SUPPORTING LEADERS—COACHING YOUR TEAM TO WIN!

What is a coach? A coach is a person who helps you get from point A to point B. He or she helps you reach your goals.

Coaching is more about listening and asking questions than giving advice. Coaches help small group leaders analyze their problems, brainstorm options, find solutions, and make decisions. Beyond that, an important part of coaching is to come alongside small group leaders and be their friend and help them implement their long-term plans.

Coaches can help small group leaders set and achieve some specific goals, including deepening the leader's walk, resolving conflict, raising up an apprentice leader, assimilating new members into the group, pushing group members into new areas of growth, or multiplying the group.

The most effective coaches are those who put their leaders first by doing the following:

✦ **Pray.** Nothing tops this. Leaders who are prayed for deeply know it. Prayer encourages the heart and soul of small group leaders. Leaders, in turn, pray for each of their small group members.

✦ Love. Leaders need coaches who truly care about them, who love them as brothers and sisters in Christ. That may include "speaking the truth," but leaders can hear the hard truth their coaches say because they speak it "in love." Leaders trust that what is said will help them grow spiritually and make them better leaders.

✦ I Listen. Nothing says "I love you" like someone who listens and truly hears your concerns. Coaches need to ask questions to discern where leaders are in their faith walk and their life stage. What outward circumstances are impacting them? What are the wounded places in their lives? What needs nurturing and care? The question, "How are you doing, really?" says it all. Listening and really hearing someone says, *"I truly care about you, not just what you can do for our small group ministry."*

✦ Resource. Leaders also need someone to navigate the maze of small group resources, from training and conferences to books and study materials. Providing a book review or synopsis of a training event via e-mail is time efficient and frees the leader to concentrate on his or her group's needs. It also provides guidance as to what resources to utilize, what training to pursue, and what to disregard.

✦ Provide individualized support. Not all leaders need the same kind of support. Relational leaders need affirmation and talk time. They are people-focused. They also need simple, practical organizational tools—assistance with what they are not good at—so they can maximize the people skills that they possess. Task-oriented leaders thrive on organizational structure, goals, and objectives. They are action-oriented and want a measurable, concrete "to do" list from their coaches so they can do their jobs better. They also need simple, practical tools for connecting with people—which may not come naturally to them—so they can utilize what they do best and still remain people-focused. Both relational and task-oriented leaders thrive on the praise and encouragement of their coaches, but for different things. Coaches need to recognize that their own needs may be different from their small group leaders, and they need to support the leaders according to what the leaders need, not what they themselves need.

✦ Respect and trust. Leaders need coaches who respect what God is doing in and through their small groups and their leadership, coaches who trust God's call in the leaders' lives. It includes trusting leaders to discern where their small groups are in their life cycles and allowing the leaders and the groups to determine when they are ready for a new agenda and when they should reproduce or even end. Trust frees leaders from the burden of performance; respect empowers them to pursue their God-given passions and process.

✦ Encourage spiritual accountability. Coaches who empower and release small group leaders to follow the Holy Spirit's leading emphasize spiritual accountability instead of positional authority and control. It means that both the leader and the coach mutually submit to an agreed upon vision for small groups. They walk side-by-side, holding leadership loosely and hanging on tightly to God. When they live out the "one anothers" of the New Testament, God pours out his blessing. Then, even in the tough times of group life, leaders and coaches will see God at work.

Train your coaches to provide that kind of support. It will give your leaders what they need most—guidance for doing God's will.

—Source: Betty Veldman Wieland, SmallGroups.com

IS IT WORKING? CHECKING SPIRITUAL HEALTH

I have found that people evaluate "small group health" from very different perspectives depending on their roles in small group ministry. When small group directors, staff pastors, or leadership boards talk about small group health, they talk in terms of uniform measurements (percentage of people in groups, development of new group leaders, retention of existing small group leaders, percentage of leaders who actively participate in training events, number of leader coaches, and so on). Additionally, I've noticed that church leaders often measure group health based on what they do not hear (the old idea that no news is good news—the absence of news bubbling to the surface about relational conflict, divisions, shaky doctrine, poorly shepherded members, and other issues).

Small group leaders evaluate small group health from a very different perspective. Many group leaders do understand their role in the bigger church mission and vision. However, the health concerns and "measurements" are very different.

Because of the different perspectives depending on where you function in the overall ministry structure, broad diagnosis of small group health is needed. That broad diagnosis, I believe, involves three unique levels of assessment:

> **From "I'm not being fed" to "I'm not growing."**
>
> I used to hear it all the time—"I'm just not being fed in this group" or "I'm just not being fed by this curriculum."
>
> Perhaps statements like that were being driven by a very consumer-oriented mind-set of a decade or so ago. Today, I don't hear that line nearly as much as I used to. Instead I'm hearing, "I'm not growing." People say it in various ways: "I've been going to a Bible study, but I haven't bonded with anyone there …" or "I think I would like to try a different group…" The problem is not knowledge—they've been fed plenty. It is that all that spoon-feeding has not really satisfied and nourished to the point of growth.
>
> Growth is not about gaining knowledge. Information intake has been so abundant and easy that people are starting to feel fat and lazy and not healthy and growing. That is why today I see more people craving growth through discovering their purpose and mission in life. They perceive that what really helps is when they burn some of those knowledge-fed calories in service and actually love someone more than they used to.
>
> Leader adjustment: Help your groups understand that the reason they've not been feeling well is that they have been bingeing on information. What they are really craving is a spiritual workout of service and mission. Help them to not just look in the mirror, but to do something about what they see (James 1:22-25).
>
> —Source: D. L., SmallGroups.com

❶ **Spiritual vitality of the group and group leader(s)**

❷ **Spiritual health of the group members and their relationships within the small group community**

❸ **The health and effectiveness of the small group ministry within the whole church**

Look at each level based on the core values of the ministry to see how well those values are being lived out at each level.

TOP 10

REASONS THE PASTOR IS VISITING YOUR GROUP THIS WEEK

10. His wife's out of town … and he can't cook.

9. Several members of your group recently appeared on Jerry Springer.

8. He wants to get out of his own group for once.

7. He just found out the church has a small group ministry.

6. Your small group is watching the NCAA Tournament for a community building exercise.

5. He's curious about your study of "Origami and the Bible."

4. Juicy sermon illustrations.

3. Heard you were taking an offering.

2. He somehow got a hold of the refreshment list and always happens to show up on pizza night.

1. Was curious when he heard your group has a building fund.

(Source: SmallGroups.com)

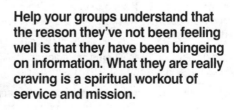

Help your groups understand that the reason they've not been feeling well is that they have been bingeing on information. What they are really craving is a spiritual workout of service and mission.

REMEMBER...

From Program to Process. Relationship is the key ingredient in healthy spirituality—relationship with God and with one another. Relationship is a process-driven enterprise. People are rejecting the notion that they can program their spirituality using four spiritual laws, three easy steps, 40 days, or whatever. Today, they want to know how to "join you on the journey," rather than "get with the program."

Leader adjustment: If you are program-oriented, shift the emphasis from completing the program to joining the journey and hold relational ministry as your highest group value (Acts 2:42-47).

—Source: D. L., SmallGroups.com

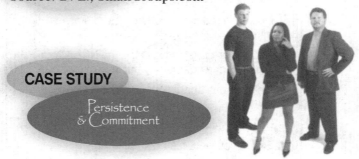

CASE STUDY

Persistence
& Commitment

July 26, 2001, was the fulfillment of a dream for Brett Noble. Testimonies. Covenant making. Prayer. And food—lots of food. Brett had overcome incredible odds to give birth to a small group. And now he was enjoying a well-deserved birthday party.

Brett's small group was one of the five that had started in an initial burst of excitement in 1999. But the excitement died when the pastor left, dividing the church in the process. Brett's group managed somehow to survive, while the others died slow deaths. And now Brett, the lone survivor, was celebrating the fulfillment of a dream.

As we gathered in Brett's home in Redlands, California, to celebrate, we rejoiced in a mission accomplished, a dream fulfilled.

But I'm sure many, especially those with a long history at Brookside Chapel, were wondering, "Why Brett?" He seemed shy, even reserved. "What did

Brett do differently from the leaders who fell along the wayside?" As I talked with Brett, two things became crystal clear.

Persistence

Brett persisted. Even when the pastor left, Brett knew that God wanted his group to grow and be fruitful. Knowing this, he pressed ahead, seeking to honor God. "It was tiring," he confessed. "I really didn't know what I was doing. At times we would go for weeks and weeks, and the meetings seemed so unfruitful."

"But each time that I got to the point of quitting, I heard the Lord say, "Be patient; I will do it in my time." While the others dropped out, Brett kept his ear attentive to the voice of God, knowing that God had called him to lead the group. "It's amazing to me that my group is multiplying," he said. "God has truly done wonderful things."

Commitment

Brett also asked for a commitment from the group. "For a long time," Brett said, "people would come and go. The group would grow larger, then smaller. This became very frustrating."

"Finally, I realized that I had to ask the core group for a commitment. I asked the group to come each week and to commit themselves to each other. Now," Brett said, "if someone is absent, they'll call and tell me they can't make it."

Brett developed a strong core. Yet he didn't stop there. He persisted to point the group toward the goal of multiplication. Eventually, Timothy, a computer programmer, committed himself to lead the new group.

I saw in Timothy many of the same qualities that Brett possessed: dependence on God, persistence, and commitment. "I don't really know what I'm doing," Timothy said to me, "but I believe that God wants me to lead this new group."

Christ-followers who are not necessarily talented, gifted, or outgoing but who continue to reach out have one thing in common. They don't give up. They are persistent and committed. They keep on encouraging small group members to grow and reach out, even when the results are few. They keep on praying, even though the answer is not immediate. Remember the Scripture in Proverbs 14:23: *"All hard work brings a profit, but mere talk leads only to poverty."* Such diligence will lead to success eventually.

—Source: Joel Comiskey, SmallGroups.com

DON'T GIVE UP

Starting a vital small group ministry is a difficult, daunting goal for most. And it should be. It's a God-sized goal and requires a long push in the same direction.

What it boils down to is that to start and grow a small group ministry you must count the cost of discipleship. It requires a persistence, commitment, and dependence on God that many in the church have lost.

The path to Christian community is the way of the cross. But remember—there's hope on the other side. Ask Jesus. Don't give up. You'll discover the fulfillment of your hopes and dreams, if you persist to the end.

NOTES

CHECK OUT THIS VAUABLE COUPON!

FREE

SMALL GROUP RESOURCES

For MORE HELP, check out the small group leader resources on *SmallGroups.com*.

With the purchase of this book, you are entitled to a free one-month membership at *www.SmallGroups.com*. To claim your **FREE** membership:

➤ Go to: *www.SmallGroups.com/freemembership*.

➤ Continue through "checkout" process.

➤ Select payment method "check/money order." However, no payment is due if you use coupon code: **stdsg06**

➤ Then click "Redeem" and "Confirm Order" for your free membership!

Redeem your coupon *today!*